11 Secrets of Nonprofit Excellence

11 Secrets of Nonprofit Excellence

Merger, Transformation, and Growth

Kathleen Stauffer, MPA

BEP
BUSINESS EXPERT PRESS
Leader in applied, concise business books

11 Secrets of Nonprofit Excellence: Merger, Transformation, and Growth

First published in 2023 by
Business Expert Press, LLC
222 East 46th Street, New York, NY 10017
www.businessexpertpress.com

ISBN-13: 978-1-63742-465-0 (paperback)
ISBN-13: 978-1-63742-466-7 (e-book)

Business Expert Press Human Resource Management and Organizational Behavior Collection

First edition: 2023

10 9 8 7 6 5 4 3 2 1

For Rick DeMatto, an excellent mentor to many—and an excellent friend to so many more.

Description

Bridge the Knowledge Gap

Do you have what it takes to build agile, successful teams? Pursue mergers that transform? Are you solving the right problems for efficiency and growth? Do you want to leverage your mission for large-scale social change? Does your Board have a shared vision for innovation?

Discover the critical lessons of success with *11 Secrets of Nonprofit Excellence* in this step-by-step executive guide:

- Build effective, enthusiastic teams;
- Deploy tech to boost revenues and quality;
- Launch profitable microbusinesses;
- Negotiate game-changing legislative outcomes;
- Design and implement dynamic strategic plans.

11 Secrets offers practical stories, disciplines, data, and humor in an empowering blueprint for achieving excellence in any organization. The book addresses the resource gap for navigating nonprofit growth and innovative tech solutions. Deftly weaving vignettes from the author's successful careers in international publishing and nonprofits, *11 Secrets* introduces real-life encounters with notables such as Muhammad Ali to unlock valuable secrets of quality, excellence, and mission advancement. *11 Secrets* lends itself to powerful coaching and winning outcomes for start-ups, nonprofits, boards and leaders, cross-sector.

Keywords

nonprofit; excellence; leadership; team building; crisis management; merger; social change; nonprofit tech; jobs IDD; microbusiness; poverty of expectation

Contents

Testimonials

"Peter Drucker first identified the importance of studying nonprofit management. 'No Margin, No Mission' is one famous quote. Nonprofits are by far the largest employer group in the U.S., and they are the original laboratory for managing knowledge workers. Kathleen Stauffer has added valuable insights to the store of knowledge in this field. Ms. Stauffer's 11 Secrets lives in the real-world of experience, and I find that her insights are also relevant to some of the start-ups that I work with."—**Hugh Evans, Founder and Managing Member, 3D Ventures**

"Kathleen Stauffer has written the blueprint for creating, managing, and advancing a successful and thriving nonprofit. Really, if you have a business of any kind this book is a must-read. The strategies in this book will not only take you to the top but will keep you there."—**David Perozzi, Senior Producer, CNN**

"11 Secrets of Nonprofit Excellence provides invaluable insight into different styles of leadership and how to become a successful leader in the nonprofit world. One of the most valuable leadership tips given is 'Get up from your desk!' See from the front-line perspective what are the impeding issues and welcome the truth from your people as a gift toward the resolution of an issue and a giant step toward progress."—**Shiela Hayes, President, NAACP Norwich Branch**

"This book will prove very useful to nonprofit leaders because its storytelling provides a universal platform for its insights. In addition, its lessons are user friendly and defined. Kathleen Stauffer's method of highlighting both takeaways and questions is extremely helpful also. Overall, I will be referring to this book regularly. It is an excellent work that ties direct human experiences to critical tools for managing."—**Win Evarts, Executive Director, The Arc Connecticut**

Disclaimer

While all details of this book are based on fact, anecdotes, people, or places created from composites have been designated with an asterisk (*). Any resemblance to individuals, living or dead, specific places or events is strictly coincidental.

Acknowledgments

With appreciation. When then-president of the board of directors of The Arc New London County Rick DeMatto suggested I write this book, I laughed him off. But Rick brought the idea up again and again. The conversation continued after board meetings, between seminars at conventions and—once, even—while sipping chilled martinis amid an ocean breeze. Nobody was more masterful at mixing work and fun than Rick. So, to Rick goes the credit for envisioning, with joy, what I had not. For the careful reading and loving encouragement while I wrote this book, I thank my spouse, Kimberly Theidon, whose own beautiful prose and important books inspire people the world over. Also, thanks to The Arc Eastern Connecticut's Board President Diane Aubin, Vice President Gene Michael Deary, Treasurer Shannon Aiello, Secretary Ray Baribeault Jr., and Past-President Linda Rhodes. But for the support and singular vision of the agency's executive committee and its entire board of directors, I would never have written this book, let alone done so during an international pandemic. I also thank my expert C-Suite: Annemarie Bellenoit (another careful reader of the book), Scott Kadey (who contributed the book's graphics and an insightful interview for the technology chapter), Laurie Herring (another supportive reader), Terry Hickey, Bill Furgueson, and Denisse Mateo. Your strength and compassion throughout COVID and several mergers have themselves been lessons in excellence for me. Working beside people of talent and integrity, folks who believe in excellence as a means to empowerment, is a blessing few enjoy as I have.

A long time ago, an English teacher named Lesley Huss Misko believed in me, encouraged me and—not unlike Rick—badgered me (for decades!) to write more. So, thank you, Lesley and Bob Misko for remaining friends and allies all these years.

Though Bob Misko passed away in 2021 and Rick DeMatto in 2022—the legacies of those who teach and inspire are eternal. I still hear your affirming voices, and it reminds me just how much good people matter in this world.

I also thank Rick Wilber, author and poet, who helped me to focus this book, as did others: Alnoor Ebrahim, Professor of Management at the Fletcher School and Tisch College of Civic Life at Tufts University; inclusive housing developer Sheldon Bustow; and Crown Publishing author and realtor Nancy Kahan. Fellow Board member of The Arc of the United States Hugh Evans suggested capturing the Secrets at the end of each chapter and steered me toward the phrase "A poverty of expectation." Hugh believes that Elise McMillan, Past-President of The Arc of the United States, coined the phrase. And to the professor who proved I really can "do" math, I acknowledge Professor Charlie Coleman, University of New Haven, whose bureaucracy lessons significantly inform this work. *Finally, to my mother, who signed the papers and to the family members who've been there ... thanks.*

SPECIAL GRATITUDE to Katy Giffault, my delightful editor, marketer, and friend in food who pulled stories from the middle and put them up front, brought me cover concepts ... and helped with so many things. You arrived with ideas, connections, laughter, jam—and even the right brand of sesame oil. Few have such charm and talent! To Scott Isenberg and the talented team at Business Expert Press—thank you for your belief in this project and for your creatively practical approach to visioning, marketing, and distributing new ideas. Kudos to Charlene Kronstedt for the incredible cover design. Thanks also to Dr. Michael Provitera for the keen insights for bringing everything together.

My Unexpected Journey...

Service to others is the rent we pay for our room here on earth.
—Muhammad Ali to a cub reporter, 1980

I grew up in Barto, PA, in a fieldstone farmhouse on a wooded hill where my ancestors had lived for more than 100 years. My father was born in a similar house, also hand-hewn from common rock, down a lane off the same road. Unlike our own, which was set back just a little from the street, the house of my father's birth lay shrouded beneath a stand of massive conifers whose limbs reached so high that, as a child, I thought they really did touch the sky. My father's mother was born across the field in a brick house that could be seen from the porch of my childhood home.

Having attended the Henry Ford College of Engineering, courtesy of the United States Navy during World War II, my father returned home from the South Pacific Theatre, married my mother, and proceeded to automate the factory that employed him in the town at the bottom of our hill. My father's bent for creation didn't stop when he came home from work. He and my mother wanted a large family, so he built a kitchen with a table that had a hidden, expanding leaf that could be pulled forth to enlarge our dining space as the family grew.

Photo courtesy of Genevieve Gehman

Because he thought it would be fun, he built an enormous see saw that went up and down and around in circles. Nine or 10 children could easily sit across its length, and we often did—my own six brothers and sisters joined by cousins or children from around the neighborhood. Our sandbox was approximately 8 feet square, with bench seats so all of us could sit around the sandpile and play together. My brother, Biff*, now an architect, would subdivide the sandbox, build streets, and assign lots. Deep into the mechanics of patting my own little crumbling house into a square, I'd look up and see him polishing the walls of a multiwinged ranch with crisp sand lines and a fully landscaped yard—complete with a swimming pool at the back.

We never worried about our father losing his job, and we never went to bed hungry. We had gardens and orchards, and each summer brought an abundance of wax beans, lettuces, green beans, sweet corn, plump tomatoes and peaches, and cherries and plums. Lots of people envied us, but I suspect that some of us harbored resentments. I know I did.

My parents were children of the Great Depression. My mother's family was so poor she had rickets as a child, a Vitamin-D deficiency sometimes linked to malnutrition. My father's father, Marvin, owned a truck farm and refused to use banks his entire life because The Run during the Great Depression convinced him that banks couldn't be trusted.

In our family, the roots of poverty's psychology ran deep. At some point during my youth, an older cousin, Winston*, stopped by my grandfather Marvin's place to chat. When he couldn't find Marvin inside the farmhouse, Winston began poking around the barn and the dilapidated outbuildings dotting the property. As he rounded the great barn, a yellow gambrel-styled structure, and walked toward the meadow, he spied my grandfather leaning deep into the trunk of a broken-down jalopy.

Marvin was meticulously wiping the mold off each silver certificate he was going to have to cart to the bank. The United States was moving to the gold standard, and bearers of silver notes had a window of time to redeem them. Marvin had $30,000 in silver notes hidden in the trunk of that old black junker. He also owned a robust stock portfolio. Yet Marvin's farmhouse, in 1971, had no indoor plumbing or central heat.

What everyone imagined to be an idyllic life lived on a bucolic hill in Southeastern Pennsylvania was, in fact, a hardscrabble childhood scarred by a profound, pervasive fear of poverty nursed in the souls of the adults around me. Yes, there are many wonderful memories and lessons that turned me into the person writing this book. Yet I was only 10 or so years old when I stood in a blazing heat in the middle of a row of yellow wax beans and vowed to leave town when I turned 18. I had no idea how it was going to happen, but I was going to write books for a living. I had a lot of stories living in my head, and none of them involved wax beans.

I was 8 or 10 or so when I told my father that I wanted to go to college to become a writer, and he laughed. "I'm not wasting money educating a woman," he said.

I thought he was joking. But after I won a full scholarship to Point Park University in Pittsburgh in the Fall of 1980, he was no happier. My high school faculty celebrated, but not my dad. As it turned out, his resistance had nothing to do with the cost of a college education. Because I was 17, I needed parental consent to accept the award. Yet my father refused to sign the papers receiving the scholarship on my behalf. In the only moment of marital defiance that I can recall, my mother signed them instead. And off I went—my father grumbling all the way up the PA Turnpike as he drove me and my box of possessions to Pittsburgh in the family station wagon.

My father loved me. I believe that he did want happiness for me; however, a mindset of poverty, a poverty of expectation, left him unable to imagine a world capable of celebrating one's dreams fulfilled. The specter of poverty that overshadowed his own childhood led him to fear my dreams would turn out poorly for me even if they did come true.

Some five years later, having bumped around covering high school news, courts, and features for our hometown weekly in the same station wagon that drove me off to college, I graduated with a bachelor's in Journalism. By then I had written for the *Pittsburgh Press* and completed a summer stint at the *Reader's Digest* surviving the same internship that had inspired Sylvia Plath to write *The Bell Jar*. With a sniff over lunch one day in Chappaqua, New York, one of the *RD* editors complained about the intern who wrote that "awful little book" cautioning us over a lunch of lamb chops and white wine spritzers not to drink the contents of our fingerbowls. She needn't have worried. Even someone hailing from Barto, PA, knew better than to pluck the violets from a finger bowl and slurp the water.

My ticket out of Barto was a red Plymouth Horizon bought in nearby Quakertown for $6,212. Following graduation and a Sigma Delta Chi Award for an article written for the *Pittsburgh Press* about fathers who failed to pay child support, many packets with my sample writing clips went forth by mail from Barto, to publications nationwide. I was job hunting. My father told me I'd never hear anything back, and why would we waste money on postage like that?

A telephone interview from the editor-in-chief of *Faith Journal** came out of the blue one afternoon while I recovered from a wisdom tooth extraction. My father shook his head in disbelief when I told him I'd landed a job, then gifted me the money for the Plymouth Horizon.

I drove off to South Lake*, KS*, in that little red car to embrace my first full-time editing job. Journalism gigs were getting hard to come by, and I felt lucky to find work that allowed me to read all day, put my *Reader's Digest* condensation talents to use and earn $12,000 a year to boot.

There were no Rodin sculptures in the foyer of *Faith Journal* as there had been back at *Reader's Digest*. But because the bottom had yet to drop out of periodicals publishing completely (even though advertising dollars were getting harder to come by), we did enjoy a largesse of martini lunches and festive holiday parties at the Lawn & Pond Club* in South Lake for quite a few years. My career progressed, and I was promoted.

Only in hindsight do I realize my next 30 years were spent in an industry that wallowed in a poverty of expectation. Like the never-ending rows of wax beans and weeds and the sun that beat down on Barto, PA, delivering a life I hadn't chosen and sought to escape, we watched as *Faith Journal's* circulation trickled downward each successive year. Advertising sales dropped just a little bit more annually along with the circulation declines.

By now a young executive-level editor, I recognized the challenge the Internet posed to print publishing. I had been a college student when cable television clobbered the networks. Yet time after time, people in the business office at *Faith Journal* eschewed online investment. It was universal, industrywide. My friends who worked at other publications and even my little sister who by now was a daily newspaper editor on the East Coast, would sit around over wines and beers and sushi reciting the same lament. Why didn't the older generation of publishers understand the importance of investing in the Internet? The response, throughout publishing, was consistent if uninspired: "We don't have the money."

One publisher would retire, and another would take his place (in those days publishers were men, Katharine Graham notwithstanding). With each new publisher, the editorial department or the newsroom would energize. Maybe this fellow would get it. But publishers began to come and go like seasons—a few like lambs, most like lions—and still circulations and ad dollars eroded steadily.

It's often the case that we are oblivious to the themes of our childhood until as adults the patterns of the past allow us to run in circles no longer. My psychological acceptance of a poverty of expectation as an excuse for a general lack of progress notwithstanding, by the time I turned 30, I had figured out that "What will it cost?" is the sledgehammer of creativity.

One new publisher arrived with fanfare, in a custom-made suit amid rumors that he'd negotiated the highest salary in the state. I say fanfare because his new office furniture arrived before he did. Within a few days of ensconcing himself, R. Bud Whipple* began to hold endless meetings. Editors grumbled that it was difficult to do the job because whole days were getting eaten by meeting attendance and entire weeks with meeting preparation.

R. Bud was looking for new ideas, and that seemed hopeful to me. Finally, somebody was going to do something about the Internet. R. Bud called all of us into his office. He wanted to know what we were thinking and what we thought might stave off our eroding print circulation.

"Well, I think people are always going to read print," I told him. "But I think we need to invest in the Internet."

R. Bud's eyes glazed over. "What will it cost?" he said.

CHAPTER 1

Trust Your Gut

I didn't have the ability to vocalize in my childhood the gnawing apprehensions weighing upon me. Today, I believe our family was often paralyzed by fears rooted in the Great Depression, decades earlier. Even now, I struggle with spontaneity. Anything worth doing must be planned and strategized and then planned and strategized again ... right?

Not true. Living through a great crisis might leave us thinking that we can avoid future trauma by endless planning and endless preventive action, but sometimes unexpected things just happen. At such times, success is measured not by how much planning we've done. It's measured by how resilient we are, and how quickly we adapt. Strategy matters, and so does innovation on-the-fly.

In the mid-1990s, with journalists from around the country, I spent a week at the Poynter Institute for Media Studies in St. Petersburg, Florida, learning the craft of writing from the world's best editors, men and women who worked at *Rolling Stone, Time, Inc., Newsweek, The Philadelphia Inquirer, The St. Petersburg Times*, and more.

We learned that every great story is much like a movie in the making. The prose of your opening paragraph either starts with a close-up and then pans to a wide-angle view, or you begin with the wide angle and move in for the close-up.

How executives manage their own job searches and careers often mirrors the way they build teams and companies: Some CEOs are all about the wide angle, while others are all about the close-up. In fact, success requires a bit of both. Truly successful outcomes, moreover, require that we know the difference between when the close-up (details) or the wide-angle (big picture) is needed.

During my final years in publishing, when I mused about doing something completely different (although I didn't think I'd actually end up doing something completely different), I understood America was in the midst of a Great Recession, and it might be safer to stay where I was. When The Arc New London County called, I wasn't all that interested because I believed that taking on something completely new held great risk, particularly at that point in economic time. The change in my thinking otherwise was gradual.

For one thing, I'd done all of the jobs in publishing to which I'd aspired: editing, writing, publication design, marketing, advertising, sales, strategizing, publishing, and publicizing. I was in my mid-40s—did I really want to do the same thing for 20 more years? The publishing industry had failed to adapt. Salaries were stagnant. I'd catch myself thinking that working this hard in any other profession was bound to be more lucrative. But then I'd think: *Do I really want to start over?*

One Saturday morning in 2007, as I paid the household bills, I gazed out the window into my garden. Bright green ferns fanned upward along a small, fenced-in hill with stands of thin oaks and maples stretching as far as I could see. The thought was fleeting, but it was clear, and it gripped my fancy sufficiently to still remember it after all these years. *Should I stick with publishing?* If anybody had told me that afternoon that, before two years had passed, I'd be walking away from publishing for good, I would have laughed.

People usually look at risk and think, "What can I gain by acting?" But sometimes greater risk lies in what we stand to lose by inaction. When The Arc called, one could have argued that much of my career in publishing lay ahead: I'd gotten a call from the *Los Angeles Times* once, but in the end didn't really want to live in LA on a journalist's salary. An emissary for a small chain of newspapers in Florida had called the week before I accepted a job at The Arc to say, "I'm moving on, and the publisher's job is yours if you want it." A senior executive in an international corporation, I had been working in publishing for 30 years. I could choose my next step. Wouldn't it be safer to stick with what I knew?

As a lark that Saturday afternoon I'd created a document on my computer's desktop. If I were to leave publishing, what kind of opportunity might justify that risk? Whimsically, I created a checklist. For several successive Saturdays, for my own amusement, after I'd paid the bills, I'd reopen the document file (now called "The List") and add and subtract things as they struck my fancy. Satisfied the "must haves" were complete,

I began a second column. This one contained all the things about being a publisher that were less to my liking, things like downsizing (basically, laying people off), answering to corporate authorities for plans I'd had no hand in crafting, and working 70-hour weeks.

The List Looked Like This

THE LIST

REQUIRED . . .	DEAL BREAKERS . . .
☐ Job with values-based mission allowing me to help make the world a better place	☐ Fulltime fundraising
☐ CEO level job with benevolent employer	☐ Struggling corporation
☐ Job that exercises all my talents	☐ Selling dues, subscriptions, memberships
☐ Latitude to run things optimally	☐ Aging brand
☐ Nonprofit?	☐ Job that requires me to work even more than I do now
☐ Job in higher education or supportive of my own educational investment	☐ Publishing, marketing consulting (might as well stay put!)
☐ A business with one or more businesses within it	☐ Faith-based organization
☐ Entrepreneurial opportunity	☐ Fulltime writing job
☐ Appropriate use of skillsets	☐ Fun job that doesn't actually make a difference in the world
☐ Nice people	☐ Old-fashioned business model or leadership averse to change
☐ Easy commute	☐ Organization with no IT department or understanding of critical value in the modern era
☐ Interesting work	☐ Job with nasty politics or leadership that won't allow cleaning up the place
☐ Government contract revenues if nonprofit	☐ Dishonest people
☐ Government service?	
☐ Product with robust demand	
☐ Location, Southeastern CT	
☐ 6 figures or potential within 3 years or much reduced responsibility/hours to justify	
☐ Good healthcare and other benefits	
☐ Trusting leadership that allows me to come and go with professional integrity rather than engage in meaningless busywork	

DESIGN BY
Scott Kavky

I had no way of knowing, as I wrote The List, that The Arc NLC's Board of Directors was on a similar journey of discernment, asking: *What does our future look like? What will it take to navigate the challenges of the future? Should we be a large agency or a small one? What kind of leader do we need?*

Problem solving and decision making amid unknown risks, like the questions facing The Arc NLC's Board of Directors, are among the greatest challenges leaders face. Nonprofit and for-profit boards of directors, executives, mid-level leaders—indeed, even governments and politicians and individuals—face similar risks every day. One can say that risk and leadership go hand in hand. Often, the risks involve dollars and cents, but just as often they involve human prospects, too.

In the 1990s, *Faith Journal* sent me on a press trip to Turkey to write a travel article. Imagine walking in the footsteps of the Apostle Paul, witnessing real-life whirling dervishes, the intricately tiled palaces of the Sultans, and enjoying the stuffed peppers, dates, and figs favored by the Ottoman Turks (horsemen who liked their food to go). For 10 days running a contingent of fellow journalists and I, guests of the Turkish government, enjoyed geological sights, archeological wonders, and amazing dishes. After dinner each night, belly dancers with castanets clicked strong coffee and dessert into banquet rooms.

One afternoon, Bernard McDonagh, author of *Blue Guide to Turkey*, and I found ourselves on flat, brightly painted benches six inches off the ground. Sipping cups of weak Turkish tea, we sat together shopping for colorful, handmade carpets in an Istanbul bazaar. Early the next morning, Bernard and I and the rest of our contingent were back on our tour buses. All of us were writers from international magazines and newspapers brought to Turkey by its tourism bureau in hopes we'd share tales of the Arabian nights and more with the readers of our U.S. and international publications.

From Istanbul we were whisked toward Turkey's interior, Ankara, and then to points south. As our buses glided onto a southbound highway leading to Adana, arguably home to the world's tastiest kebabs, night fell. I slept while we drove. As most of our party snoozed, a few began experiencing Traveler's Gut. Sticking to bottled water and cooked restaurant meals (on the advice of a colleague) had served me well, but before long an ambulance pulled beside one of our buses and our caravan bumped off the road and onto a dusty berm. Somebody in the back of the bus was going to need urgent care, and we wished him well as the paramedics took over. We were reassured he'd be fine, but his dehydrated body needed fluid replenishment requiring medical intervention.

By now, the cities of Istanbul and Ankara had melted into a verdant countryside filled with night sounds and plum-colored shadows.

The toilet on our bus had failed, and everybody filed out when we stopped, some from necessity and others in search of fresh air. We found ourselves in a meadow running purple with moonlight. Deep in the middle of Turkey, between Ankara and Adana, far from the artificial lights of urbanity, the night sky glowed true Cobalt Blue. All 9,096 stars in the universe, fixed in space, shimmered there as if someone had tossed a handful of diamonds skyward, where they stuck, like so many pinpoints of light.

Chck-Chckck! The unmistakable rack of semiautomatic weapons breached my reverie. A Turkish army platoon, rifles turned toward the violet mountains that rose up, up, up from the edges of the expansive field where we stood, had fanned out in circular fashion, protectively, around us. I turned to the burly, bespectacled bald guy beside me, a reporter from the *Baltimore Sun*. "What's with the army regiment?"

He shrugged. "They say there's a bad guy up in those hills. He'd like nothing more than to kidnap a contingent of international journalists to make a name for himself."

"Who says?"

The man shrugged again, "the CIA, according to our bureau guys."

"What's his name?"

The reporter gave me a name I'd never heard before and added, "He's a terrorist."

"Seriously?"

"Well, a wannabe terrorist, at least …."

We laughed.

"Oh, what's he gonna' do, really?" I smirked. And we chuckled again while re-boarding the bus. As dawn broke, our bus pulled over amid grassy terrain. As we climbed off the bus, we looked around in confusion. Why were we stopping? Though the distant mountains and dusty rugged landscape were beautiful enough, I could discern no newsworthy sites nearby: No mosques, no ruins, no people.

I turned to one of my travel buddies, an editor from *Guideposts*. "There's nothing out there!" I said.

"C'mon," she replied, it's over here.

About 20 yards from our press corps buses lay a ravine looking very much like a dusty, inverse volcano. Everything about the scene gave me pause. "We're going down *there*?"

"The children in the village are putting on a play," my friend said and began carefully picking her way downward, along the rocky, buff-colored path that led down, down, down to the village. I began following but, after a few steps, stopped. We were walking into an abyss, and it felt dangerous.

About 15 feet ahead, even deeper into the cavernous decline, my colleague looked up. "You're not coming?"

"I don't know," I told her. As seatmates on the bus that morning, I'd relayed the story *The Sun* reporter had shared some hours before about the wanna-be terrorist up in the hills. We'd kind of joked about it. Now, I wasn't laughing anymore. "If there really are terrorists up in those hills," I told her, "even Mossad won't get us out of here."

My colleague walked a few more steps, paused, looked downward, turned, and began a return to the bus. "I'm not going either," she said.

Barely had she crested the rim of the ravine when, with lots of dust and lots of yelling, a fleet of camouflage Jeeps flew toward us, stones flying as they skidded to a stop. The Turkish army had returned. With frantic motions, the soldiers herded all of us back to our buses, which hauled out of there as fast as the top-heavy vehicles could fly.

On returning stateside, magazine stories filed and published, I forgot about that odd interlude of Jeeps, shouting soldiers, tour buses lurching at high speed and the bad guy who might have been up in the hills. Deadlines and routine busyness set in. Two years went by.

Like almost everyone else in the world, I awoke on September 11, 2001, wholly unaware. I do recall sitting at my desk and looking out my office window, which overlooked a manicured courtyard on the Institute of St. Dismas* campus in South Lake, where our magazine was housed. The statuesque elms spread their leafy branches toward a perfect sky, and I remember thinking how calm and blue everything was.

In a few short hours, I was sitting in shock in the *Faith Journal* boardroom watching the Twin Towers burn. Manny*, a young assistant, turned to me. "Are we going to have a war?"

The innocence of his question jarred me. Without thinking, I responded with words I still regret, unfiltered, honest, too analytical—but very journalistic. "Manny," I told him, "We *are* at war. We are under attack. *This is war!*"

Manny began to cry. Awkwardly, I tried to walk him back from distress while CNN began reporting a new lead:

Intelligence officials believe these bombings to be the work of al-Qaeda, an extremist group founded by a wealthy sheikh named Osama bin Laden....

Where had I heard that name before? And then, slowly, like a book read long ago, memory leafed back the pages. I recalled that beautiful night on the way to Adana when the stars seemed to dance in the sky and the meadows and the mountains glowed purple beneath a cobalt night sky....

"*What's with the army regiment?*"

"*There's a bad guy up in those hills. He'd like nothing more than to kidnap a contingent of international journalists....*"

"*What's his name?*"

"*Osama bin Laden....*"

Was Osama bin Laden really in the mountains of Turkey back then? I have no idea, and this tale isn't intended to imply that he was. It's a true story, nevertheless.

Leadership is all about strategy and intuition: Make the best decisions you can with the information you have. Anticipate trouble. Neutralize it or convert it into opportunity when you can. Build a team and make sure that team has the training, resources, and direction it needs. Set a tone of respect, collaboration, and optimism for the organization. Encourage your team to lead with confidence in turn. Lynda Applegate, Baker Foundation Professor at Harvard University's Business School, is fond of saying, "Hope is not a strategy!" In fact, instinct is not a strategy either, but if you and your team have done the work of strategizing, then your instincts will serve you well.

And ... never, ever, walk into the ravine with your team if your gut tells you not to do it! The reverse, by the way, also is true. If you have the odd feeling that life is passing you by, that there must be more to life than rows upon rows of wax beans—well, then, be assured that there is.

The Secrets of Chapter 1

- TRUST YOUR GUT. What are your instincts telling you? What are your concerns? What is the evidence for your concerns? Better yet, what opportunities do you see? Write them down....
- TAKE RISKS. Based on the evidence you see, what actions or decisions might you logically take to ensure better performance? What aspects of these actions or decisions hold risk? What can you do to mitigate risk and optimize opportunity?
- BUILD A STRATEGY. Strategies are action plans. Every action plan requires a series of steps or goals. The best strategies involve both evidence-based action steps and intuitive action steps all mapped out via a series of successive goals.

For Discussion

- COST VERSUS OPPORTUNITY. Have you or an organization you've worked for avoided taking risks because of cost? What was the result? Might you (or they) have made a different decision? How and why?
- ACTING ON OPPORTUNITY WITH INTUITION AND SMARTS. Is there one thing in your life or your career that you very much want to happen? What are the three action steps that might help to make that opportunity a reality? Write them down. Take care to ensure the steps of your plan are both evidence-based and intuitive. *Now, take action!*

CHAPTER 2

Unlock the Genius of Your Team

One of my most impressive mentors was a dashing manager whose courtly personality, unceasing smiles, and flair fed his popularity inside and outside the company. I learned to smile my way into meetings by watching him. Keeping a door open when it might otherwise have closed … another lesson learned by observing this guy in action.

From finessing to dressing well to solving budding problems *really fast*—each of these invaluable skills would be absent from my executive skillset had this man never crossed my path. In hushed tones, everyone from assistants to lieutenants and division heads acknowledged Franklin's* genius. My own memories remain fond, although I came to see his legacy differently as mentors and coaches became more numerous and diverse across my career, cross sector.

Despite Franklin's brilliance, for example, the corporate bottom line remained lackluster. The sheen of Franklin never rubbed off on the results. Each time we came close to pulling up the nose of the plane, we'd glance off in another direction and all the zip would evaporate from our momentum.

It was frustrating and draining. Each time it happened, I wondered: *Why? Why could we never quite get to our goals?* Everyone wondered. Even Franklin.

In all the years I knew him, Franklin's dashing façade cracked only twice.

The annual holiday party had been booked, as usual, in one of the best restaurants in town. Team members arrived jovial and with anticipatory excitement, in part because this was traditionally a time for and a means of conveying good news. After a brief speech of thanks and recaps of our accomplishments, the group leader would then hand out our incentives.

Some years would be better than others, but as the recession loomed and the publishing industry plunged into an ever greater crisis, we had a streak of weak results.

Nobody gave up, though. Despite the disappointment, we gamely kept on. We assumed that if we just kept trying, the tide would turn.

The weather was warm for a winter's day. One by one, our cars wound up a short stone drive toward an Alhambra-style mansion overlooking Lake Leonard*, a large reservoir in a small southwestern town*. Christmas trees decorated with Victorian angels flanked lead-paned windows framed by brocade velvet drapes. An ornate, hand-carved staircase lazily curving to the ceiling led to the second-floor guest rooms of the inn.

These were the decades of spirit-laden holiday parties that, for so many reasons, have fallen out of favor. Drinks in hand, departments self-segregated. A lively hum fed by restrained laughter and ice cubes clinking against glass expanded in the festive room.

Expectations fueled by the impending holidays and hopes of bonuses hung in the air with the mistletoe. Every face was wrapped in a smile as Franklin stood to address us. But Franklin's own smile dimmed, and he grew increasingly pensive as he commenced speaking. It had not been a good year, again. Franklin stood there before us, in his fine suit. Absent was his omnipresent smile. As he spoke, Franklin began to sound like "not-Franklin."

Apparently, a lot of people had asked Franklin about the bonuses this year, and he found it irritating. As he spoke, his pitch and agitation rose.

There would be no bonuses.

The room's mood sank like a souffle pulled from an oven before its time.

But Franklin was just getting started.

"There will be no bonuses! There will be no raises!

"There will be no vacations. There will be NO REWARDS. NOTHING. *Nothing!* Until. Revenues. INCREASE!"

By now, Franklin was grimacing and pounding the table. Crystal and silverware jangled.

"There MUST be a complete turnaround!"

Franklin did not say how we were to accomplish a turnaround or what, exactly, each of us needed to do to make it happen.

He was quite clear about one thing: He wanted us to *work*. And work some more. Franklin did not explain how we needed to work, what specific goals were to be achieved by working, or by what means or with what resources such change might be accomplished.

Feeling like misbehaved children, we stood amid the festive tables and fine china, with sweeping water views shimmering beyond an expansive, manicured lawn. Franklin ranted on about our lack of profit, and when he finished, lunch was served. Stuffed flounder and prime rib and bread and butter were masticated in funereal fashion.

The following morning, back at the office, we discovered Franklin wasn't done.

He called the executive team into the boardroom. Anyone who'd hoped to find him remorseful was disappointed. Franklin began scolding us again. So inflamed was he that, as his ranting gathered momentum, blood began squirting from his nose.

Franklin stopped only to snatch a proffered tissue. He waved away the box. His back to us, Franklin dabbed at his nose. Each time he yelled, blood spurted anew until, finally, with a fleeting suggestion of humility, he accepted an adequate tissue supply, box and all.

The idea that teams perform stronger than individuals is not new. Yet, despite all the valuable lessons Franklin taught me and countless others throughout his career, he himself had failed to grasp a critical one: Teams are smarter than individuals. The lone genius theory, the company's top-down notion that Franklin's genius would save us all, was a myth.

Not only do teams outperform individuals 66 percent of the time, but the more diverse the team, the better its performance. Diversity of age, gender, and geography improves decision-making outcomes 87 percent of the time (Larson 2017).

For all his smarts, Franklin had a way of preventing innovation. "There is a blind spot in leadership, management, and social change," C. Otto Scharmer writes in *The Essentials of Theory U.*

> It is a blind spot that also applies to our everyday social experience. The blind spot concerns the inner place—the source—from which we operate when we act, communicate, perceive or think. We can see *what* we do (results). We can see *how* we do it (process). But we usually are not aware of the *who:* the inner place or *source* from which we operate. (Scharmer 2018)

There are ways to tap into that source. Scharmer outlines a methodology for drawing forth inspired solutions: It is called Theory U. Working from a process of listening, inclusion, and enlightenment, Theory U offers a path for elevating the genius of the team rather than that of the individual. The process map, shaped like the letter U, inspires the name. The bottom line? Great leaders, leaders who know how to build excellent teams and lead those teams to excellent results, know how to Make Space for Creation.

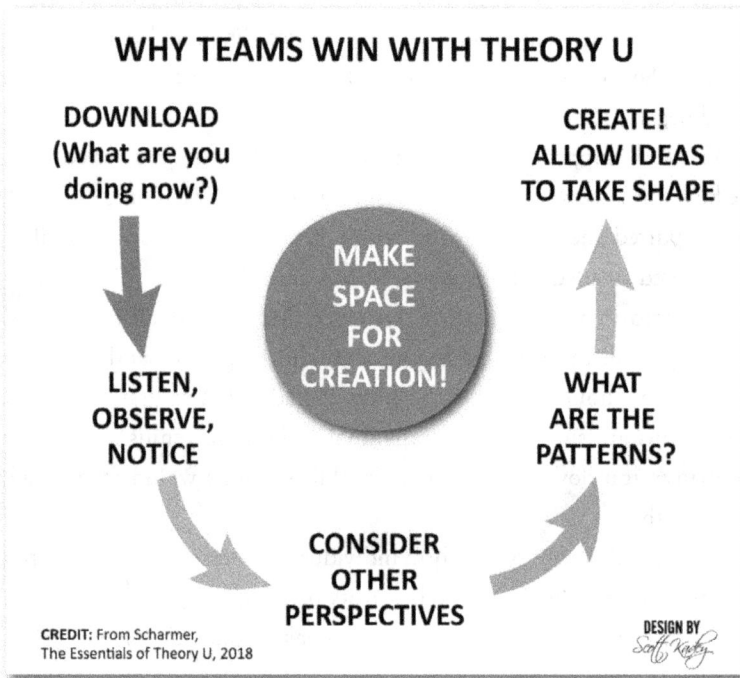

WHY TEAMS WIN WITH THEORY U

DOWNLOAD
(What are you
doing now?)

CREATE!
ALLOW IDEAS
TO TAKE SHAPE

MAKE
SPACE
FOR
CREATION!

LISTEN,
OBSERVE,
NOTICE

WHAT
ARE THE
PATTERNS?

CONSIDER
OTHER
PERSPECTIVES

CREDIT: From Scharmer,
The Essentials of Theory U, 2018

DESIGN BY
Scott Kinley

Dazzling as working for Franklin could be, it was frustrating and demoralizing, too. Just as the team was about to make a breakthrough, Franklin would sweep in and change the plan. He was, after all, the genius from whom the corporation derived its mojo. Scharmer explains why the cultural presumption that Franklin's genius would carry the day was a lie: "What counts is not only what leaders do and how they do it but also their 'interior condition'—that is, their inner source (Scharmer 2018)." Alas, Franklin, skilled in so many ways, was unable to give our team a safe space to create.

Imagine working in a vacuum for an entire lifetime. This is how our company functioned–in the vacuum of Franklin's mind. If new ideas entered the workflow, they came from Franklin and were communicated by Franklin. If new products were to be introduced, they would resemble ones that had proven profitable in the past or were profitable for one of our competitors. We could only create things that were like things we already made, or things Franklin had discovered in his far-flung quests, or products made by companies Franklin had acquired by convincing Wolfe Westin*, our company's proprietor, were worthy investments.

Though Franklin badgered us *constantly* to create something completely different, he invariably dismissed ideas that didn't resemble what we already had because the newer concepts had not yet proven themselves capable of profit; sometimes, I thought maybe he just didn't get what we were pitching him because he wasn't really listening to our ideas. In any case, he was not providing an environment conducive to creation. In fact, we felt neither safe nor creatively empowered.

Doing the same thing over and over in the same way, of course, even if the result has been stellar in the past, doesn't guarantee perpetual or future success. If anything, it ensures stagnation.

Excellence in leadership, like an agricultural combine, requires that we cover as much ground as possible, channeling the highest quality ideas into the appropriate bins to optimize harvest. This is what we mean by "a safe space for creation." It requires an inclusive mindset, a team mindset—and, also, a mindset capable of appreciating diverse insights. Inclusive leadership brings out the best talents of each group member and organizes and channels them, thereby enhancing the organizational mission and the operational bottom line. This, in turn, fuels careers where professional growth can be promoted and rewarded. It's also about planful coaching, ensuring that people have a safe place not only to create but also to solve problems. These conditions, then, nurture and grow performance. Achieving excellence offers a certain balance to risk because excellent leaders surround themselves with excellent teams. Excellent teams are winning teams.

High-performing teams are confident teams made up of members who look out for one another, teach one another, inspire one another, and learn from one another. All of this mitigates risk while contributing to that critical "safe space" so essential to productive, creative teams. Looking out for one another doesn't necessarily mean we always agree. It does mean we respect our colleagues' ideas and do what we can to elevate the brainstorming process.

Franklin frequently gave detailed orders, left town, and returned just as the team prepared to launch a service or product. He'd look at the plan, built exactly to his specifications, and—as if he'd never seen it before—demand extensive changes. Keep in mind, the original plan was *his* plan! Over time, I noticed that even when his initial ideas appeared fresh and different, or whenever he took input from someone else on the team (which wasn't often), the retooling always looped us back to virtually the same prosaic place, resulting in the usual, tired outcomes.

"Do it this way!"

Franklin was literal. If he said, "Do it this way," he really meant do it *this way*. If somebody on the team perceived that a part of what Franklin envisioned needed adjustment, I would dread having the conversation with him.

Never punish your employees for telling you the truth. When your team tells you the truth, they are giving you a gift.

Telling Franklin that our seasoned customer service representatives had made thoughtful observations based on what they knew about our consumer base only brought forth his wrath. Because we were serving multiple demographic regions, Franklin was a living example of why diversity and respect for intercultural difference really matter. He often insisted on processes that—while successful in one area just wouldn't translate to another.

Whenever it fell to me to convey to Franklin constructive suggestions from the team or to explain that things were done that way in this particular region or that one, I had the distinct sense that my career was on the line. Franklin's displeasure was obvious. Doing the right thing—telling Franklin the truth—became terrifying.

And so I learned a powerful lesson: *Never punish your employees for telling you the truth.* When your team tells you the truth, they are giving you a gift.

Over time, the thrill of working for a genius like Franklin wore thin. I found myself sitting at my desk thinking: *What if I were to do something completely different?* It was a musing borne of frustration, infrequent and niggling. It was the source of my introspection as I found myself paying the household bills that Saturday, a few years prior to exiting a field I'd loved all my life.

Perhaps it was foreshadowing. When the phone call came, albeit out of the blue and unexpectedly, the timing was right. My friend Tom seemed to think I might be a perfect fit for a nonprofit leadership job.

After a couple of friendly conversations and exchanges in which I indicated clearly that I did not think I was a very good fit for the job, I finally agreed to take a closer look at the proposition my friend had laid out. Franklin had often said he was grooming me to be a chief executive officer. In fact, I felt ready to be a CEO.

But I didn't want to work with Franklin anymore.

In many ways, Franklin had been an extremely generous mentor. Franklin was cunning, and he'd taught me to watch my back. Franklin likewise had taught me many invaluable lessons about process and product delivery. And yet, like a beloved sports franchise that never quite wins the championship but clinches division after division title, Franklin's psyche always got in the way of the big win. It puzzled, perplexed, and fascinated me.

When Scharmer references the "interior condition" of leadership, the power of his imagery grows clear. Franklin was a smart and often generous man. He taught our team valuable lessons about getting things done and getting them done well; about reading people; about delivering products through complicated processes and obstacles. But for all his trolling far and wide for innovation and new ideas, Franklin would forever be a team of one, stuck in his own private loop. Franklin, I now suspect, was nursing his own deep poverty of expectation.

There was something frantic about his quest for the perfect product and the perfect performance. No thought was given, though, to the inner condition of the individuals or the team. Rather than a planful, interactive exploration, Franklin seemed obsessed with individualized busywork. Nonstop work. Frantic work. "The job is 24/7!" he had lectured one new executive. By insisting on frenetically crushing, relentless industry,

Franklin taught me not only the dangers of insular thinking but also the dangers of workaholism and burnout.

First, as noted, we never clinched the Big Win. We worked and worked and worked. Then, we worked some more. Through the years, I watched my co-workers get sick: autoimmune disorders, cancers, and rare ailments. Even the employees themselves remarked on it.

A turning point came after I was chastised for taking a second one-week vacation (I was eligible for six weeks of vacation per year) to attend my niece's wedding in Alta, UT. I hadn't ever done it before, but a year prior, I'd alerted corporate that I'd be taking a second week (about six months apart from my usual week) for a family wedding. Usually, I took one week annually and forfeited the other five because I was too busy to get away. About two weeks prior to leaving for a trip I'd planned for a year, corporate set a critical strategy meeting in a Midwest state the day after I was to return. As a division president, I wasn't a newcomer wanting to be coddled. I had asked a year in advance if that particular week of the year would pose a problem and if any corporate meetings had been scheduled for that time. I'd been reassured that it was fine. (And then, it seems, Franklin promptly forgot he had given clearance.)

But something was different about this vacation. Normally driven and driven to perfectionism, I gave myself permission to handle this one in a new way. I felt comfortable that I had professionally cleared the time. I did what I could to ensure the appropriate reports would be prepared in my absence. I was aware by now that co-workers were getting sick, and—if I could help it—I wasn't going to drive myself (or my colleagues) to illness, too. I had also reached a point where, as committed as I was to great performance, I felt I had a right to a personal life as well. Franklin's relentlessness, and ours, wasn't leading to improved outcomes. There had to be a better way. I was trying to find my way to it.

Amid the languid rise of the snow-capped Wasatch Mountains in Utah, sweet strains of a ukulele's plucking *Over the Rainbow* alighted upon the wedding party in the little mountain village of Alta. On my brother-in-law Ron's arm, my beautiful niece Hannah promenaded across a patio bathed in sunshine to stand beside her groom, Josh. Hannah and her father Ron walked together down the aisle while Josh waited.

The greens of a Utah spring surrounded the touching scene. Sweeping plains of snow cut into the meadows with dazzling white swaths. Above us hung an expanse of soul blue sky. It seemed perfect, but it was the perfection that only one moment can bring.

Less than a year later, my brother-in-law Ron, Hannah's father, had died. The life of the man who had taught me to throw a softball properly when I was 12, who played guitar and sang like Bob Dylan, who built intricate bird houses that welcomed bluebirds and goldfinches to my backyard, was celebrated by a standing-room-only crowd in a country church in Pennsylvania.

The man whose safe driving was often the source of family anecdotes was traveling home from work, less than a mile from the little hobby farm he'd so lovingly tended, when his pickup truck was slammed head-on by an erratic driver. Two Life Star helicopters were dispatched. Ron's was turned back shortly after touching off from the ground. He had passed quickly. The other driver died aboard the other Life Star on his way to the hospital. Route 6 in north central Pennsylvania was shut down in both directions for six hours. The accident was front page news for a couple of days.

In the odd way that grief sometimes brings clarity, I now felt defiant about that vacation.

And that's why, when my friend Tom called several times to say that a nonprofit agency on the East Coast was looking for a CEO and he thought the job was perfect for me, I finally responded, "Tell me more...."

Tom's daughter, Mary, had Down syndrome. Mary herself died when she was just 15. Tom felt passionately about The Arc, an agency serving people with intellectual and developmental disabilities (IDD), people like Mary.

The more I learned about The Arc NLC, the more I realized its mission was something I could believe in. Although I had no human service experience, Tom—a community banking executive—insisted that I send him my resume, which he would pass along to the nonprofit. Finally, I complied, saying, "But you have to tell them that I'm wholly unqualified to do this job!"

"They want someone who can run a business," Tom said. "And, it has to be a businessperson with a heart! You are perfect for this job!"

What I didn't know back in 2009 was that The Arc Eastern Connecticut had found itself at a crossroads. A beloved executive director was retiring, and the board of directors of what was then The Arc NLC convened to discuss the agency's future (Stauffer 2019).

The volunteer board of directors recognized that the agency was neither large nor small. They knew change lay ahead, and they acknowledged it. Technology would be crucial to the agency's success, they knew, and they believed The Arc had little expertise in it. They weren't sure how things stood financially, but they did know that new approaches and efficiencies would be needed regardless of the direction they chose.

Change was coming, and the Board decided it wanted a leader who could do more than cope. The Board wanted The Arc to thrive, and they agreed to commit to change even though they weren't sure what the answers to many of the questions associated with the challenges that lay ahead might be. The Arc needed a change agent as its next chief executive, somebody who would bring a fresh perspective and strong leadership skills to unlock the genius of teams. The directors resolved that it was more important to find a person who matched this description than someone who had expertise in the field of developmental disabilities.

Having clarified the questions that lay ahead, The Arc's Directors sent word forth in the community, and in doing so, they clarified what kind of person they wanted to interview. That's when my phone rang.

I knew nothing about the story of intellectual disability and only a little about society's profound rejection of people who had intellectual disabilities. I was honest about that, and I found it perplexing that so many people—from The Arc's Board of Directors to its many community partners—responded to my protestations with the same sentence: "Yes, but you *care*!"

Before long, I discovered that one word unites the disability community unlike any other, and not for any good reason: *Willowbrook.*

With fascination, I watched a video from that dreary winter morning in 1972, when a young reporter named Geraldo Rivera leapt a fence on Staten Island with a news crew from WABC in tow. Using a stolen key and acting on a tip, the young lawyer-turned-reporter and his team entered Building #6 of the Willowbrook State School, an institution for people with IDD (London 2016).

More than 40 years later, Rivera grows emotional recounting the memory, saying he'd been warned Willowbrook's conditions were bad, and still he was hardly prepared for what he found. "It was horrible."

"It was called a school, but there was no education. It smelled of filth, disease, and death. [The residents] were making a mournful sound, a pitiful wail," he says. "The biggest abuse was the concept that you could mass produce care of the disabled the way you made Ford motorcars, on an assembly line" (Rivera 2016).

"There was no effort," Rivera said. "We don't even know what these kids are capable of."

A young graduate school student at Columbia University, the late Rick DeMatto, was sent to Willowbrook with his class the day after Geraldo broke in. A past board president of The Arc ECT's Board of Directors (then The Arc NLC), DeMatto recounts his own haunting recollection of Willowbrook. "People were naked, sitting on the floor. To clean the place, they just hosed it down, people and all, with a drain in the middle of the room." DeMatto told me the story several times. He told it with tears in his eyes every time.

Vanessa Leigh DeBello, author of *Moron: A Daughter's Story of an Accidental Childhood in Willowbrook*, told National Public Radio (NPR) that her mother spent 16 years in Willowbrook after a test pegged her IQ at 53. "The legacy of Willowbrook remained alive in DeBello's mother," according to NPR. "DeBello says her mother was always dressed poorly, even years after her discharge when she was married and had children. DeBello says she never achieved a sense of self-worth. 'Take the credit card,' her husband would say. 'Go, buy something!'" (National Public Radio 2008). But she never did.

Willowbrook had instilled a mindset, a poverty of expectation, deep inside her, shrouding the woman's ability to acknowledge even her basic needs. Some years ago, I visited Southbury Training School, one of a handful of institutions remaining in Connecticut. Once again, The Arc Connecticut—an advocacy organization for people with IDD and the agencies that serve them—was pushing the state to honor its court-ordered obligation to alert the residents of a state-run institution called Southbury of their right to live in community settings following a court ruling via Messier versus Southbury Training School (Messier v. Southbury Training Sch., No. 3:94-cv-01706 (VAB) (D. Conn. Aug. 31, 2018) 2018) decades before. The Arc and various human service providers were invited to Southbury for a housing fair: Residents and families living in Southbury were being offered community living options around the state.

But like Vanessa DeBello's mother, many did not have an informed opinion of their options. Years of institutional living had left people with the sense that Southbury was all they had. Some Connecticut residents did not even know they had relatives living in Southbury. One woman and her husband stopped by our booth to pick up brochures and avail themselves of information. "My father died years ago," the woman said. "My mother died a few months ago. And we received a letter in the mail just like that, out of the blue! 'You have a brother!' the letter said. All these years, my sister and I thought it was just us two. And now we discover we are three!" She began to cry. "I only met him a couple of weeks ago for the first time. He was older than we are. We could have known him all these years! I am so angry at my parents for doing that to him and to us, for depriving us of one another all these years. He … is … one … of … us! *He's family!*"

The stigma of IDD often results in a poverty of expectation for families grappling with the challenges of IDD. In years gone by, medical professionals counseled parents that their children had no intellectual prospects, often for no reason other than their IQs were low or because physical challenges stigmatized children and schools denied them a formal education.

My own grandparents were pressured time and again to put my aunt in Wernersville State Hospital, in PA. My aunt had acute epilepsy, and when she was about eight or nine years old, the elementary school principal at the school she attended called my grandparents. "You have to pick her up," he said. "She falls down and has these fits. She scares the other children, and it disrupts their lessons. We can't have that at our school anymore."

As she got older, my aunt's epilepsy grew much worse. Medical advisers continuously advised institutionalization. My maternal grandfather, a dairy farmer and factory worker, and my maternal grandmother, a homemaker, were finally persuaded. It's a story my mother told me many years ago: One day, a visitor stopped at the family farm for a friendly chat. The conversation turned toward Wernersville. The visitor casually noted that women "patients" in Wernersville were getting pregnant. "Nobody knows how."

My mother says her father wordlessly walked away from the conversation and into the farmhouse. He picked up his car keys, got into their car, and drove away. When he returned, my aunt was in the car. "I don't need a college degree to know that Wernersville is no good for my daughter," my grandfather announced. And he gave word that my aunt—no matter what—was never, ever returning to Wernersville. And she did not.

While our family's poverty of expectation ended in one respect that day, it lived on for the rest of us in other ways. One key to achieving success in life—be it in our personal or our professional lives—requires that we keenly identify areas where we are clinging to false truths or misreading our options. Once we have identified these areas, we can then dare to achieve greater outcomes. We can embrace a vision of what might yet be. In this way, we open the door to opportunity, yes, but also to improved outcomes for ourselves—a manifestation of excellence in our lives. In the workplace, we can accomplish it by establishing a safe place to create. Only then can we build a team, grow a vision, and leverage our missions, be they personal or professional, for good.

The Secrets of Chapter 2

- POVERTY OF EXPECTATION. To attain excellence, lead with vision, not with cost. Excessive emphasis on cost; misreading the challenge at hand; clinging to false truth (i.e., "That child cannot learn.")—all are manifestations of a poverty of expectation. The antidote? We need to ask the right question: What will it take to achieve our desired goals?
- DARE TO BE GREAT. Excellence springs from mission, vision, and bold expectations. "What will it cost?" is the sledge-hammer of creativity. Write a few phrases you might use to open a discussion around innovation rather than shutting it down with "we can't afford that." Next time you are tempted to shut

down a conversation by citing cost, nurture creativity instead with one of these phrases. Over time, it will become a habit.

- UNLOCK THE GENIUS OF TEAMS. Are you a change agent? What perspective(s) do you have that qualify as fresh and innovative? What are your leadership strengths? Write a few leadership strengths that you want to grow so you might better become a more inspiring leader, better able to unlock the genius of your team.

For Discussion

- EVALUATE. How well does your team work together? How can you work together to transform the dynamic? List a few areas where you can support your team in growing a more collaborative spirit.
- GROW VISION. Have you or has your company ever suffered from a poverty of expectation? How? What might be done to avoid making the same mistake in the future?
- GROW MISSION. What prompts can you build into your procedures and processes to avoid the trap (and the excuse!) of embracing a poverty of expectation in the future?

CHAPTER 3

Create a Trust Equation

The summer following my hire at The Arc, I was in Reno, Nevada, attending a Leadership Training Institute sponsored by The National Conference of Executives of The Arc. Fresh from Franklin's tutelage, I eagerly took notes as Beth Jandernoa of the Presencing Institute of Cambridge, MA, offered to local executives of The Arc from across the country a seminar called, "Leading for Profound Change and Innovation."

"If you do what you've done in the past over and over again," Jandernoa noted, "it doesn't seem to work. So what skills, abilities, leadership are needed to create profound change?" (Jandernoa 2010). Immediately, I thought of Franklin.

Jandernoa introduced me to the framework and methodology for eliciting a phenomenon of deeper awareness and creativity called *Theory U*. As I listened, I was amazed at how accurately Theory U explained Franklin's failed quests for success, and his great frustration.

The brainchild of Massachusetts Institute of Technology lecturer C. Otto Scharmer, "Theory U focuses on how individuals, groups, and organizations can sense and actualize their highest future potential" (Scharmer 2018).

In *The Essentials of Theory U*, Scharmer points out that the same material responds very differently under contrasting conditions. For example, water is liquid; but, as ice, it is solid. The variable is temperature. "One of my most important insights is that there is a blind spot in learning and leadership," Scharmer writes. "This blind spot concerns the sources from which our action and perception originate. **The aim of the Theory U method is to orient our attention to the *sources* of action and thought** (Emphasis Scharmer's). Our patterns of thinking, conversing, and organizing create a global world of social complexity that we enact moment to moment. How can we investigate the process of creating social reality? How can we catch the process of social reality creation in flight?" (Scharmer 2018).

Scharmer challenges leaders to facilitate environments that nurture people in ways that allow us to see something new, *to create*. If water can be ice, and ice water, *then the conditions make all the difference!*

Franklin, as a leader, needed to ensure that the atmosphere of our workplace facilitated the desired outcomes. Metaphorically speaking, Franklin was complaining about ice while keeping the temperature at 32 degrees Fahrenheit. Blaming employees for ice when a company sets the thermostat at 32 degrees doesn't work for people, and therefore it doesn't work for creation.

An enhanced diagram of Scharmer's Theory U looks like this:

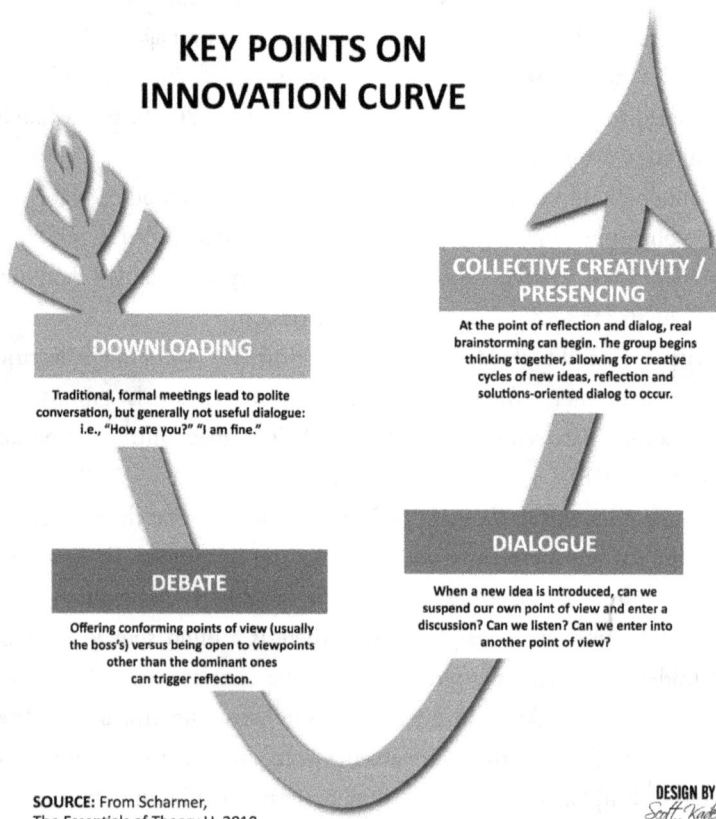

KEY POINTS ON INNOVATION CURVE

COLLECTIVE CREATIVITY / PRESENCING

At the point of reflection and dialog, real brainstorming can begin. The group begins thinking together, allowing for creative cycles of new ideas, reflection and solutions-oriented dialog to occur.

DOWNLOADING

Traditional, formal meetings lead to polite conversation, but generally not useful dialogue: i.e., "How are you?" "I am fine."

DIALOGUE

When a new idea is introduced, can we suspend our own point of view and enter a discussion? Can we listen? Can we enter into another point of view?

DEBATE

Offering conforming points of view (usually the boss's) versus being open to viewpoints other than the dominant ones can trigger reflection.

SOURCE: From Scharmer, The Essentials of Theory U, 2018

DESIGN BY
Scott Kadey

Not only are the conditions of productivity and creativity critical to optimal problem-solving and excellence, the collective psychology of a workplace is equally important. Looking at the diagram, we can see that Franklin pretty much stopped at "Downloading." **Yet, setting a stage for positive outcomes requires an environment facilitative of team building, discussion, brainstorming, and cocreating. Employees need to feel safe and free to take risks.** *Indeed, in the workplace, people need to feel support from their co-workers in sufficient quantity so as to feel safe even if they fail!*

A primary obstacle to innovation in the workplace, in fact, is the fear of failure. Amy Edmondson, in her book *teaming*, explains why:

> Most of us have been primed to aim for success .... And so, people at work often remain silent about the potentially informative mistakes, problems or disappointments they've experienced, which means that companies miss the learning that could be gained from failures. This barrier to learning from failure is rooted in the strong psychological and social reactions that most people have to failing. Self-serving biases that bolster self-confidence and protect one's public image make these barriers even stronger. And natural biases and their corresponding emotions are exacerbated by most organizations' inclination to punish failure, as well as by the strong connection between the concepts of failure and fault. (Edmondson 2012)

Even before taking on positions of corporate leadership, I disliked the word "fault." Something goes wrong in a department or a company, and everybody wastes time proving why it isn't their fault even as the problem at hand goes unsolved. **Yet the real work, ideally, is analytical: What happened? What needs to happen to attain the desired outcome? A truly excellent workplace, then, employs real problem-solving played out via an expression and practice of virtue in the classical sense: honesty, respectful feedback, trust, trustworthiness, teamwork.**

As a leader, one of the most important things you can do for your team is build a culture free of blame and fault. In a social service agency, where matters of life and death play out daily—medicine administration, compromised immune systems that introduce potentially lethal conditions without warning, exacting food preparation guidelines, varying types of human mobility and communication—eliminating notions of "fault" and "blame" as a means of establishing a culture of excellence might seem counterintuitive. If something goes wrong, shouldn't the responsible parties be held accountable?

Yes, and there are differences between blame and fault and responsibility. Responsibility is a virtue. Blame is not. Only when people have the confidence, the trust, to ask the questions that lead to greater knowledge, to seek support, and to provide support to one another (responsibility!) can each team member rise to a greater level of competency or excellence. Only after each team member understands that learning is more important than being right, will the group be free to embrace the virtues that make for team excellence: a sense of personal responsibility, honesty, generosity, helpfulness, and humility. Teams must actualize beyond the narrow pursuit of personal self-interest, also known as CYA, or Cover Your Ass.

TRUST EQUATION

−fault

−failure

−blame

+trusting

+having confidence

+being humble

+discussing

+being clear

+being respectful

+experimenting

= Excellence/Success

DESIGN BY
Scott Kirby

I call this the Trust Equation. Team members need to embrace the greater good in ways that allow the experienced to take the inexperienced under their wing. And even experienced team members need to have enough humility to say, "I made a mistake" and then take responsibility for fixing what needs correction or, perhaps more important, asking for help in doing so. I emphasize to my team that we're all on a journey of learning and excellence and nobody is above it … not even the CEO.

One of the greatest compliments I've received came from a deputy quality assurance officer named Pat. We sometimes teased Pat that she was the mother of social work. By leading with her heart, Pat helped thousands of people change their lives for the better during her career. So, it was a great affirmation the day she said: "Do you know why we trust you? You're not afraid to admit when you're wrong. And that makes us all feel very safe."

Humility.

Edmondson maintains that organizations can be framed to facilitate optimal learning, and that this begins with leading pragmatically:

Leading Better, Leading Smarter

ACTION 1—Frame the situation for learning.
ACTION 2—Make it psychologically safe to "team," or form dynamic pods of discussion, learning, and improvement.
ACTION 3—Learn to learn from failure.
ACTION 4—Span occupational and cultural boundaries.
Source: Edmondson 2012.

While Scharmer outlines the critical need for creating an environment where groups can safely begin to think and work together as a team, what he terms the "source," Edmonson emphasizes behaviors that drive team success: speaking up, collaborating, experimenting together, reflecting via discussion and questions about processes and outcomes in a timely manner (Edmondson 2012).

Within the for-profit and nonprofit sectors, these principles are universal to excellence. In other words, excellence leads to profit, not the other way around. In the nonprofit or social sector, the word "outcomes"

LEADING BETTER, LEADING SMARTER

ACTION 1 —
Frame the situation for learning

ACTION 2 —
Make it psychologically safe to "team," or form dynamic pods of discussion, learning and improvement

ACTION 3 —
Learn to learn from failure

ACTION 4 —
Span occupational and cultural boundaries

DESIGN BY
Scott Kelby

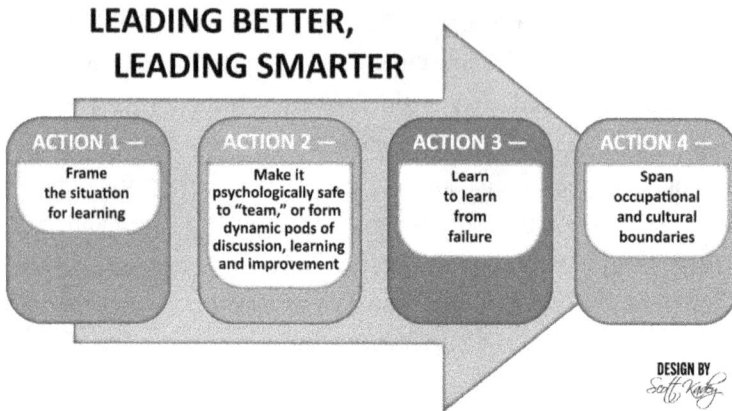

simply replaces the word "profit." A word of caution here: profit doesn't, in and of itself, mean a for-profit business is excellent any more than the mere act of service delivery guarantees excellence in nonprofit outcomes.

Jim Collins, in *Good to Great and the Social Sectors*, explains:

> We must reject the idea—well intentioned, but dead wrong—that the primary path to greatness in the social sectors is to become "more like a business." Most businesses—like most of anything else in life—fall somewhere between mediocre and good. Few are great. When you compare great companies with good ones, many widely practiced business norms turn out to correlate with mediocrity, not greatness. (Collins 2005)

So, profit isn't necessarily reflective of excellence. It simply means a business is making money. Could it make more if it were more efficient? More team-based? More diverse? Most of us probably would agree the answer is yes. But all we know about a profitable business is just that: It's profitable. It might or might not be efficient, creative, or even excellent.

For-profits and nonprofits, then, can learn a great deal from one another. Excellence translates cross-sector. "Great business corporations share more in common with great social sector organizations than they share with mediocre businesses. And the same holds in reverse," Collins notes.

> We can find pockets of greatness in nearly every difficult environment, whether it be the airline industry, education, healthcare,

social ventures or government-funded agencies.... Greatness is not a function of circumstance. Greatness, it turns out is largely a matter of conscious choice, and discipline. (Collins 2005)

In other words, excellence (or greatness) boils down to attitude, good habits, and virtue. It is the exclusive domain of neither the nonprofit nor the for-profit. Collins tells of an article where *Money Magazine* gave kudos to Southwest Airlines, among publicly traded companies, as the No. 1 company in dollar-for-dollar returns from 1972 to 2002. A $10,000 investment in Southwest in 1972 would have returned $10 million by 2002. Collins' point is that a distressed market or a distressed economy or a distressed funding source isn't really an excuse for poor performance. *(Back when I worked in publishing, none of us got that memo.)*

How, then, do good organizations become excellent ones? For that matter, how do distressed organizations move from troubled to thriving and excellent? Great leaders, leaders who have committed to the principles of excellence, need to groom leaders who likewise choose excellence. Leaders need to ensure their teams have intellectual and emotional space for dialog, listening, and innovation. Behaviors of collaboration, support, and commitment must be in ample supply.

Leaders need to provide employees with enough room to build trust so they can avoid blame and form teams and learn from one another (Edmondson calls it "teaming"). Most important, organizations need to build safety nets that allow team members to take reasonable risk without falling into an abyss. Excellent organizations, like The Arc ECT, build a healthy, dynamic, thriving Trust Equation with their teams.

The secret for creating and maintaining excellence lies in offering an environment with a safe place for making mistakes girded with systems designed with safety nets for catching mistakes and optimizing the processes of invention, intervention, and learning. Inasmuch as people can be honest with one another, virtue and excellence can prevail. Effective training programs, checklists, mentoring, coaching, and written sets of guidelines and procedures—all facilitate excellence because they guard against poor results in the face of risk. Such tools also serve as great confidence-builders for teams.

Common sense tells us that team members—at all levels of expertise—need to be chosen carefully. It goes without saying that companies take care in hiring new employees. Hiring generally takes place via a methodology. Even companies without human resource professionals or departments usually lead with applications, interviews, and reference checks. Amid these protocols, employees are hired.

That we need the right people on our team seems matter of fact, but making it happen isn't easy. Even before the Great Resignation, employers diligently sought out quality and frequently struggled to find the right people for the job.

Jim Collins explains in *Good to Great and the Social Sectors*:

> Business executives can more easily fire people and—equally important—they can use money to buy talent. Most social sector leaders, on the other hand, must rely on people underpaid relative to the private sector or, in the case of volunteers, paid not at all. Yet a finding from our research is instructive: the key variable is not how (or how much you pay, but *who* you have on the bus). The comparison companies in our research—those that failed to become great—placed greater emphasis on using incentives to "motivate" otherwise unmotivated or undisciplined people. The great companies, in contrast, focused on getting and hanging on to the right people in the first place—those who are productively neurotic, those who are *self*-motivated and *self*-disciplined, those who wake up every day, compulsively driven to do the best they can because it is simply a part of their DNA. (Collins 2005)

When I present to CEOs at seminars, something interesting happens when I talk about talent. Nearly every head in the room nods when I reference the person on the team whose performance is good, excellent in rote respects, maybe, and whose irascibility is almost intolerable for everyone in the organization. Some corporations, be they for-profit or non, have a high tolerance for misbehavior. This hesitancy may be rooted in concerns that firing a difficult person might lead to an inability to find a competent replacement. In nonprofits in particular, resource constraints can underscore this fear.

But excellence can't happen without a cohesive team. Excellence can't happen amid abusive behavior. Remember what Scharmer and Edmondson tell us about trust, learning, and a safe space to create, the so-called "interior condition." Remember The Arc ECT's Trust Equation.

One invaluable lesson Franklin taught me was how to decide whether to fire, and when. Franklin walked into my office one day and inquired about the progress of a certain project. Things weren't going well. He wanted to know why. After outlining some challenges, I asked for his advice.

"Follow me!" Franklin said with a gleam in his eye. "I will teach you how to scold somebody!"

Franklin picked up the phone and called the San Francisco* office. He fired off a string of questions. He was relentless. He asked pointed, direct questions designed to elicit clear answers. The San Fran director was known to obfuscate, equivocate, delay, make excuses, double-talk, wear everyone down with a stream of chatter, volumes of data, and veiled insults.

Franklin treated the exchange like a game. With amusement, he flipped each vague parry back to a direct question. Like a fencer, he danced his way toward the truth with small jabs. He asked one question three ways. It dawned on me he'd ask it a fourth if need be. Franklin this time did not lose his temper or even behave impatiently. He just stayed the course until he got the necessary information.

Then he barked out some orders, said goodbye genially, and hung up.

"When there's a problem," he said to me with a tone of encouragement, "don't be afraid to fix it! You are the President! Get up from your desk! Take a plane. Take a train. Get in a car. The cost of travel is small compared to the cost of failure! When you have a problem, be aggressive about fixing it!"

Basically, this time, Franklin was giving me permission to invest in outcomes. It was a freeing concept. Franklin noted that he wouldn't have solved such a problem by phone in the earlier days of his career. And he wanted me to know I had the resources to do my job in person, and that spending that money was indeed an investment.

"*Get up from your desk!*" The value of Franklin's advice is self-evident enough. The expression on the San Fran director's face when he looked up from his desk and saw me standing there, the following day, with a big smile on my face? Priceless! He never stonewalled me again. But, if he had, I would have needed to reconsider my options for that department.

"*Get up from your desk!*" It's one of the most valuable tips of my career. While I don't bark orders or snap out solutions like Franklin did, I do practice the principle of walking around, engaging people in conversation, offering advice, giving coaching tips, and often asking for advice as well. When team members offer new ideas and solutions, we do our best to implement the change—and let the person know we've done so. We try to follow up promptly, letting team members know they've made a difference within a week whenever possible.

There are, in fact, moments when I can almost hear Franklin's voice: "*Get up from your desk!*" And I always do.

The lesson has a thousand iterations, not all requiring travel. We can summon someone to our office. If the person begs off, don't allow it. Drive to the group home whose poor audit or licensing inspection just hit your desk. Look the group home leader in the eye and ask, "How can we help you with this? What resources do you need to turn things around?" Encourage the team member to see "resources" as a much bigger pool than dollars and cents. Provide reasonable supports along with a target date for completion. If possible, involve the responsible party in setting the due date so there can be no excuses should results fail to be forthcoming.

Frame your questions so the person responsible understands that facing a given challenge or solving a specific problem must be owned as part of the scope of their job. Make yourself fully available for a discussion of the problem's genesis and possible solutions: "How can we help get you back on track?" "What do you think needs to happen for us to achieve this goal?" Married with a coaching approach, Franklin's advice translates into solid leadership and a culture of excellence. Don't let problems languish. Be hands on. Empower your team.

Be pastoral. Be encouraging. Be a sounding board. Above all: *Be clear.*

At The Arc ECT, constructive criticism is a part of everyday problem-solving. As we've already agreed, confident leaders don't need to be right about everything.

This is something newcomers to The Arc ECT often struggle with even though we try to prepare recruits in advance. Too often, new hires are uncomfortable with a team environment in which theoretical solutions are met with frank conversation and unvarnished feedback. When respectful and properly facilitated, this kind of honesty leads to very good results. Rarely will one person's idea (including my own) come to fruition as initially conceived. Rather, the team will take the idea, examine it as a group, and everybody will weigh in. As the discussion progresses, the idea is refined, the process for making it a reality envisioned, and tactics for effective deployment evolved. Indeed, this is the stuff of which excellence is built, the process whereby it happens.

As a leader, you need a plan. The building blocks of that plan require taking an inventory of your organization's assets and then building a comprehensive strategy to accomplish the goals within that plan (Stauffer 2019).

The Stages of Plan-Building

Taking an inventory…

1. **PATTERNS OF FAILURE.** What and where are the systemic sources of breakdown?
2. **PATTERNS OF SUCCESS.** What are you doing right?
3. **RESOURCES OF EXCELLENCE.** What assets will it take to achieve your goals?

THE STAGES OF PLAN-BUILDING
Taking an inventory . . .

PATTERNS OF FAILURE	PATTERNS OF SUCCESS	RESOURCES OF EXCELLENCE
What and where are the systemic sources of breakdown?	What are you doing right?	What will it take to achieve your goals?

DESIGN BY
Scott Kaby

With planning, even the (seemingly) most insurmountable problems become solvable. Very few people realize how close the Allies came to *not winning* World War II. Early in the war, German U-boats were getting the better of Britain and the United States. Concerns mounted as Britain prepared to launch an expansive shipbuilding program. Before Britain had built even one ship, shortly after the United States entered the war, Franklin D. Roosevelt stunned the world by announcing America would immediately begin producing two ships per day (United States Department of Transportation n.d.).

Where did Roosevelt even come up with that idea? How might you become the kind of leader who can solve problems as complicated as a world war? Behind Roosevelt's announcement that the United States would build two ships per day is the secret to doing the "impossible," and it is a powerful lesson in leadership. Roosevelt's problem-solving methodology was fool proof:

1. **FIND TALENT.** Roosevelt firmly believed that great leaders find the smartest people out there, consult with them or hire them, and then take their advice. Roosevelt sought out the brightest, most trustworthy people he could find to advise him on solving the nation's biggest problems. He called these advisers his "brain trust," a phrase coined by his practice and still in use today (*Brain Trust* 2020). Indeed, this brain trust included the best minds, cross-industry, in America at the time. U.S. Presidents thereafter continued Roosevelt's tradition. Today, we call this body the Presidential Cabinet.

2. **FRAME THE QUESTION.** When I worked in international publishing, a mentor, referencing Voltaire, told me: "In France, we always say the smartest person in the room isn't the person who offers the best ideas or who has the best answers. The smartest person asks the best question." Roosevelt deserves a lot of credit for asking the right questions. When it looked like the Allies might lose World War II, Roosevelt did not ask, "Can we win the war?" He didn't ask, "What will it cost to win the war?" Rather, Roosevelt asked a confident question, the correct question: "How can we win the war?" (House Congressional Record 1955).

3. **LISTEN.** As the smartest people in the nation, perhaps the world, debated the answer to that question, Roosevelt listened. Many ideas were thrown into the discussion that day. Roosevelt, as Scharmer would advise, set the stage and facilitated conditions for optimal problem-solving. Having done his job, he enabled consensus: *If America built ships faster than Germany could sink them, the Allies had a very good chance of winning the war.* Again, Roosevelt asked the right question: "How many ships would that be?" Another round of debate ensued, and Roosevelt again allowed his advisers to think their most inspired thoughts. At last, the group (now functioning as a team!) agreed: If the United States could build two ships a day, we could win the war. Why two? That was the rate at which—no matter how many of our boats Germany might sink—we would be able to continue to move troops and supplies in sufficient quantity to outlast and overpower Hitler's war machine.

The process looks like this:

MAKING EXCELLENCE HAPPEN

Why what seems impossible absolutely is possible. . .

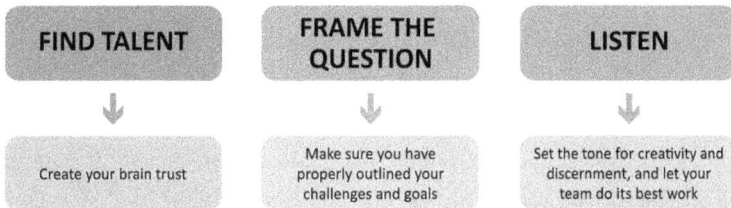

FIND TALENT	FRAME THE QUESTION	LISTEN
⬇	⬇	⬇
Create your brain trust	Make sure you have properly outlined your challenges and goals	Set the tone for creativity and discernment, and let your team do its best work

DESIGN BY
Scott Kirby

It is imperative that real problem-solving begin by asking the correct question(s), and this is true for nations, for states, for corporations, and for nonprofit enterprises (Mary Raum 2013). When I was hired by the board of directors to lead what was then The Arc NLC, this is where we began. As discussed, the board wanted a change agent, someone who would lead the agency into the future. They acknowledged they didn't know what, exactly, that meant. To be honest, in those days, I didn't either.

We did all agree on one thing: The Arc NLC needed to be an excellent agency, providing excellent services and making a public commitment of offering excellent services to the people and families it served … as well as to the community at large.

We began, then, by taking an inventory:

What Were Our Patterns of Failure?

The agency had widespread failures in documentation and procedures. The Arc's failure to document service data accurately and to train its direct support professional workforce consistently had badly hampered service delivery; and some services that were provided could not be billed out because the documentation evidencing delivery had never been done. The Arc NLC had failed to build a leadership infrastructure that knew how to document and train properly. The agency likewise had failed to nurture a team that communicated interdepartmentally. (It was high time we built a Trust Equation!)

The agency likewise had failed to conduct relevant anticipatory fiscal analysis; therefore, it had no plan for a meaningful response to an impending public funding crisis. In 2009, the world was riding roughly on the tail end of the Great Recession. But tax revenues had only begun to plummet as right-sizing pivoted the private sector into a new normal of belt-tightening and, consequently, a significantly reduced tax base for the state. This meant The Arc NLC and nonprofit state contractors like it were sure to face a funding downturn in Connecticut. Until tax revenues were again robust, and likely for a few years after, cuts were inevitable, and they were going to continue into the foreseeable future. What was our plan? *We had none, and we needed one.*

What Were Our Patterns of Success?

The good news was that the agency had done plenty of things right. The board had worked at being forward-thinking, and it had done so successfully. The agency's physical plant was well maintained and amply sized for growth. The board intended to rent out the agency's extra space for revenue. Not a bad idea. But what if we succeeded in our goal of achieving excellence? When that happened, we'd enjoy widespread demand for services, and then we'd need more space. A lot of it. It would help a great deal if we could expand quickly without needing to take on debt related to new buildings and/or space acquisition amid looming state-funding cuts—especially in light of our newly launched transformational exercises, the service growth we anticipated, and all the trainings we were going to have to do when that happened.

Another success? The board had encouraged the outgoing executive director to write grants to fund a state-of-the-art industrial kitchen via federal earmark funding. There was an understanding that people with IDD could work, wanted to work, and needed occupational training. Somehow, that kitchen would play a key role in making jobs for people with IDD happen.

Perhaps the most critical thing the board and its prior executive director had done, though, despite assessing itself as having fallen short in securing technological resources, was hire a highly competent part-time IT staffer and invest in a server.

Though inconsistent in some respects, the agency nevertheless possessed strong talents in finance, technology, and in-home supports. And, it was blessed with a board that had aspirations for the decades-old mission and vision of its founding families, the families who'd been encouraged and funded by a song-writing, country music, and movie star named Dale Evans (*more on that, and the establishment of The Arc as a national human rights movement, in the pages ahead*).

What Might Serve as Resources of Excellence?

What will it take for your organization to achieve excellence? (*Lesson Review: This is where one does not, ever, ask: "What will it cost?"*) The Arc NLC needed an operations and quality chief. It needed to build a service delivery system that produced excellent trainings and excellent service results—and an infrastructure that could then bill for those results. The Arc NLC essentially needed a highly skilled team and the resources required for excellence.

In short, The Arc NLC needed a Brain Trust. And its team members would have to be aware of the need for change and have to desire it. The team would need knowledge of the necessary changes that lay ahead, the designs for those solutions, and the abilities, talents, and necessary empowerment to implement the processes and systems required to effect change and attain excellence. The team needed training. The team needed information. More than anything, the team needed to trust its leaders to guide them on a quest for excellence (Stauffer 2019).

Like any other organization embarking on a journey of excellence, The Arc needed a plan. Per the board's insistence, the agency was about to embark upon the mother of all strategic plans. The process would require the full engagement of the agency, from the people served to the people who served them, to middle and upper leadership ranks. Particularly, and especially, it needed the guidance of its board of directors.

It is said that when John Lasseter, the chief creative officer for Walt Disney and Pixar Animation, pitched the idea of creating a short animation film to Steve jobs, Jobs replied only: "Just make it great." The delightfully visual and humorous *Tin Toy* went on to win an Academy award for Best Animated short film (Gallo 2012).

In some ways, the blessing of finding my way to the The Arc NLC and, ultimately, The Arc ECT, is that I found myself serving the rare nonprofit board of directors who had the vision to give us permission to do the same. Metaphorically, at least, they were saying: "Just make it excellent."

The Secrets of Chapter 3

- INVEST IN TALENT. Focus on job descriptions and resumes. Assess, with industry salary surveys, a fair price for the best talent you can find. Remember: Flexible schedules, hybrid work options (where possible), and creative environments all have an impact on team members' job choices and retention.
- CREATE CONSTRUCTIVELY. Frame feedback constructively. Rather than dismiss something you don't understand or see value in, ask an open-ended question: "Tell me more ..."; or, "I like the idea of x, *and* I wonder what you envision for y (the part you might be concerned is less workable)."
- LISTEN. CEOs cannot listen too much.

- ACT. Build your "Trust Equation" with your team. (It's important that people see their ideas becoming actions. Success is the best motivator.) Then, build your "Brain Trust."

For Discussion

- SAFE SPACES TO CREATE. Why is a safe space to create so important? How can you contribute to your workplace's safe creation spaces? What else might you do to contribute to your team's success?
- RESOURCES OF EXCELLENCE. What are your resources of excellence? Write them down. How might you best deploy them to optimize creativity and success for your team? What other resources might you acquire to further grow excellence and excellent results among and with your team? List three action steps toward creating a strategy for making this happen.
- CAREER ACTUALIZATION. What holds you back? List three "action-stoppers" in your personal or professional life. What might you do instead? Write three ideas for turning action-stoppers into "action starters." This is a critical step to establishing your own personal strategy to excellence.

CHAPTER 4

The Art of "Good" Change

Stuart*, the sandy-haired editor of *Faith Journal* walked into my office and handed me a pale blue post-it with a telephone extension scribbled in pencil. "Call this number."

I had no idea it was the extension for the Human Resources department at the Institute of St. Dismas in South Lake, the entity that owned our journal. Today, I'd be wiser. Then, I simply made the call with no real apprehension and was asked to stop by HR, so down the iron staircase of the converted old paper mill* I went, out the doors of *Faith Journal* and into the brilliance of a beautiful fall day.

Gold limestone buildings rose like medieval fortresses along the walkways cutting through the well-manicured lawns. Sunshine glinted off the edifices of higher education. On a stone bench outside the hulking building that housed human resources, a skinny balding man talked giddily on a cellphone. "We just bought *Faith Journal*."

Up two flights of gleaming stone stairs I went, less oblivious now. The descending numbness that heralds life's shocking moments settled upon me. An administrative assistant opened the door to a room where a beaming fellow in a double-breasted navy suit studded with gold buttons welcomed me. Spreadsheets, papers, laptops, and cardboard coffee cups littered the table. A rail-thin administrator with a Faustian mustache and a charcoal suit moved lithely back and forth among the laptops and stacked documents.

Of course, there was good news and bad—the inevitable by-product of mergers and/or acquisitions. The slant all depends on who you are, where you are in the deal's food chain and whether the professional concussion in your life is surmountable. In this case, I had a job. Although I'd need to pack and move half-way across the United States, the move would be paid for by the new owners of the *Journal*. About 60* of my co-workers were now out of work, so I certainly had no cause for complaint. But how does one navigate that state of affairs? The mood back at the *Journal* was glum indeed and knowing how to behave became ... complicated. To their credit, my co-workers were gracious. That, of course, only made me feel worse. Yet this was a sentiment I felt guilty admitting, even privately then, and even now.

Although it all happened several decades ago, the memory vividly plays and replays—especially during times of transition. Since that sunny fall day back in South Lake, I have been involved in more than seven mergers, acquisitions and/or discussions (NDAs, or nondisclosure agreements) cross-sector. I've served a range of roles in each of those deals and talks.

When people think mergers, nonprofit partnerships generally are not what come to mind. And yet, nonprofit and for-profit teams too often miss opportunities to learn from one another, particularly when it comes to sharing resources and collaborating. Contrary to common assumptions, the social sector, as the nonprofit macrocosm often is called, represents big dollars. America's 1.6 million nonprofits represent the third-largest segment of the U.S. workforce, or 10 percent (Duffin 2019; Independent Sector 2020). Our nation's foundations, charities, and nonprofits collectively constitute annual revenues of $1.98 trillion (Duffin 2019). Out of a U.S. population of 328.2 million, more than 157 million people are employed, and nearly 16 million of those workers advance nonprofit missions every day (Desilver 2019; U.S. Census Bureau 2020). The average nonprofit board hosts 16 governing members increasing the nonprofit universe by 25.6 million; in other words, some 41.6 million Americans involve themselves in nonprofit work on a regular basis. For this reason alone, excellence in the nonprofit sector matters.

There's no good reason for mergers to fail, but it happens more often than it should. Too little investment capital. Failures in cultural integration. Hubris. Fatal hiccoughs in operational integrity. Sloppy due diligence.

Mergers tend to have a bad name. They shouldn't. Properly done, mergers and/or acquisitions can be very good for products, for services, for the economy, and yes—even for people. Mergers gone wrong? Many do go south. There's no good reason for mergers to fail, but it happens far more than it should. Too little investment capital. Failures in cultural integration. Hubris. Fatal hiccoughs in operational planning. Sloppy due diligence.

Lives and careers can be built on proper mergers. Beautiful products and services and missions can be created or enhanced or acquired or leveraged for large-scale social change. For nonprofits, especially, mergers can open doors to big opportunities and much richer resources and excellent results. All these things enhance mission growth.

Properly done, mergers lead to transformation: of people, products, and legacies. That's why this is much more than a book about mergers. Every decision we make has the potential to lead to better outcomes for our organizations, our teams, and ourselves. Mergers are one aspect of calculated organizational transition, but transition (or change) alone does not in any way guarantee transformation. Too often, for-profits embrace merger because the upheaval of merger forces internal shift to happen. Too often, nonprofits run from merger out of a fear of change. Neither serves excellence, let alone customers and constituents.

Conventional wisdom says people dislike change, and people who've been on the wrong side of change have every right to be wary. Mergers and/or change initiatives that transform need not be feared. Transformational change is a wonderful, enlivening, excellent thing whether attached to a merger or an acquisition or not.

Excellence is the language of transformation. Thirty-plus years of change cross-sector and cross-industry have taught me that excellence and transformation possess inherent, dynamic powers not unlike the energy released when molecules connect or separate to create new substances. Transformation is not only about companies. Transformation is about people too. Each time The Arc ECT considers a merger, the "people" decisions are the ones we contemplate most carefully.

The ride from Mystic to Danielson, Connecticut, winds through country roads, stands of white pine, pitch pine, and massive, hovering oaks. Through the tribal lands of the Mashantucket Pequot Nation, drivers wend around small brooks and yawning ponds as deer graze among dogwoods and groves of rhododendron.

At 6:30 a.m. on January 3, 2019, a rousing sunrise lifted over the horizon as I made my way north to the Quinebaug office. The remarks

I would deliver played through my mind. The industrial psychologist from the agency's employee assistance program (EAP), would be in place by 7 a.m. The presidents of the boards of directors, one from The Arc Quinebaug Valley and one from The Arc NLC, along with the new C-Suite and me would arrive between 7 and 7:15 a.m. The rest of the team had been asked to assemble at 7:30 a.m.

All-company meetings raise eyebrows. A long time ago, in U.S. industry, employees had every hope that unplanned perks would at times appear. In the 1980s, in South Lake, one publisher called our magazine staff together of a Fall morning and magnanimously pulled a tarp off the boardroom table. Kansas City Royals World Series Champion sweatshirts*, celebrating our Major League Baseball win, were handed all around.

Those days are largely gone, and employees in some fields of work have fared far worse than others. Publishing is one: From 2000 to 2014, print advertising revenues declined by two-thirds, or 48.5 billion dollars (Weissmann 2014). After *Faith Journal* was bought and sold, those who survived the move learned soon enough not to ask for raises anymore, or to inquire about bonuses or perks. After all, we still had jobs.

Publishing aside, as I drove through the hills of Connecticut that morning, I was fully aware that the last decades had not been kind to Connecticut's human service agencies, either. As I stepped forward that cold January morning at 7:30 a.m., with the smell of fresh coffee hanging in the room where the merger would be announced, I smiled broadly and thanked everyone for coming.

In saying good morning that day, I channeled the person who'd received a pale blue post-it-note two decades before. Teams are built on trust and shared goals, a mutuality of mission and vision. Truth is a critical building block of trust. Teams thrive in safe environments where team members are free to be creative, voice opinions, discuss solutions, and work together toward optimal results. If we're going to build a winning team, we start with truth, and we build a Trust Equation. Mergers and change tend to shake that up for human beings, so truth and trust are critical places to start in building a new team.

The day we announced the creation of The Arc ECT, a merging of The Arc Quinebaug Valley in Northeastern Connecticut and The Arc NLC in

Southeastern Connecticut, a year's worth of work already was behind us: preliminary conversations, informal chats, and spirited negotiations. Both boards of directors had met multiple times to debate and inaugurate a new board. Mergers involve a great many details: Due diligence, which involves a database of information reviewed by counsel, finance, board members, and key members of the team; benefits consolidation; inventories of property and property values; hours of careful reading, haggling, planning; the building of timelines, employee assistance supports; media releases.

And yet, we always remember that people come first—and not just in services. Nothing prepares one for standing in front of dozens of employees and informing each person that his or her work-a-day world has forever changed. And absolutely nothing—nothing anywhere, not ever—prepares a person for the moment somebody says that your company or agency will no longer exist as once it did. Your world, your means, your family's life and way of living, have irrefutably and irrevocably changed.

This was foremost in my mind as I began speaking:

Our boards of directors—The Arc Quinebaug Valley and The Arc New London County—have voted formally to begin merging operations to form The Arc Eastern Connecticut starting today....

Why? The State of Connecticut believes nonprofit consolidation is needed. For this reason, in these times of budget cuts and crises, our boards have made a smart decision.

Together as The Arc Eastern Connecticut, we will become the largest chapter of The Arc in this state. We will have more influence. We will become stronger advocates for the people we serve and their families and for our team and our agency....

What, exactly, is an "Arc," or The Arc?

There was a time, about 70 years ago, that public schools turned away children with IDD, or an IQ of 70 or below. Ignorance led many educators to conclude that youngsters with IDD couldn't learn.

Angered and fully aware that their children with IDD could learn, parents all over the United States founded educational programs for their kids. Moms drove groups of children with intellectual disabilities across their neighborhoods to the zoo, to the library, and to museums. They built curricula though they never used that word. Determined parents who felt their kids were being shortchanged by America's public schools began to feel empowered with their children's progress, and they began to make legislative noise. The movement took off when Country and Western star Dale Evans wrote a book called *Angel Unaware* about her daughter, Robin Elizabeth, who had Down Syndrome. Evans donated all the book's royalties to a fledgling, national parents' organization. Today that organization is known as The Arc of the United States (Wehmeyer 2013).

Evans changed the world for people with disabilities and their families. If Dale Evans could be proud of her child and fight for Robin's right to be accepted, parents realized, well then, so could they. A couple of hundred years of stigma had been confronted in its tracks by a woman in a Miller Hat riding a quarter horse named Buttermilk. Along the way, she'd written a song called *Happy Trails*. If Dale Evans wasn't going to apologize for having a child with IDD, then *why should anyone?*

In America, there had long been shame and finger-pointing about the causes (both scientific and social) of intellectual disability, and now the doors of dialog had been thrown open by parents who were fed up with the systemic marginalization of their kids—newly empowered by none other than Roy Roger's better half, Dale Evans. The trilling star of Western movies encouraged parents to shrug off the cloak of shame, the poverty of expectation, that for so many years had dogged them. Today, after all that effort and so many years, life consistently serves up more travails than happy trails for families and people with IDD; their struggle for dignity and opportunity is a daily and too-often exhausting battle. But Dale Evans certainly raised the bar of expectation and perhaps, for the first time, introduced an alternative to the poverty of expectation that families grappling with the challenges of IDD had inherited.

Evans saw excellence as an equal-opportunity human aspiration. The grassroots, parent-founded organizations that today make up the national network of affiliated chapters of The Arc, each offering services and/or advocacy for equal inclusion for people with IDD, originally were called The ARC.

In the early days of the push for human rights for people with IDD, the ARC took its name from an acronym its founding parents created: The Association of Retarded Children. In time, the success of the movement in raising awareness among its members and the public was such that what is now called "The R Word" fell into disfavor. As people with IDD grew in awareness and empowerment, they began to push back on labels that implied their abilities were limited. Rightly, among the first fronts of resistance was the label "retarded."

Today, most people with intellectual disability prefer to be called "people with IDD." The majority of folks with IDD ask you and me to refrain from using the R Word, a word that implies stereotypical limitation for people humanly unique and singularly qualified in their own, individual ways. In the United States, we are talking about some 7.4 million people (University of Minnesota 2018).

Please note: The Arc is no longer an acronym, and this is true due to the wishes of the people we serve.

And so, on that chilly January day, having made the picturesque, hour-long drive into northern Connecticut, we were announcing that The Arc NLC and The Arc Quinebaug Valley, two affiliated agencies founded by like-minded parents who built a national network funded, in its infancy, by Dale Evans, had some big news. Our chapters were merging to form The Arc ECT, an alliance celebrating and furthering opportunities for people with IDD across half a state.

A decade prior, as a CEO newly hired to lead The Arc NLC, I'd sat in a nursing home with one of the agency's founding parents, Betty Demicco. "What was it like?" I asked her. *What was it like to be one of a handful of parents who believed children with IDD could learn, had potential, and deserved an education like every other child? What was it like to swim against the tide of public opinion—pedagogical, medical, scientific?*

"It was hard! Oh, we drove those kids everywhere!" Demicco said, remembering a day before school buses and schools were required by law to transport and educate her son, Donnie. I'd asked Betty if she understood that she'd helped to change the world. Demicco smiled broadly, and then she began to cry. "We never intended to start anything big," she told me. "All I ever wanted was a fair shake for Donnie."

"All I wanted was a fair shake for Donnie." Betty Demicco might not have intended to start anything big. But, with a single phrase, she had just handed us all the guiding principle of The Arc ECT. Even today, Question Zero for The Arc ECT—the question we ask to insulate ourselves against mission drift—is a grounding, directional True North for the agency's visional compass: *Will this lead to a fair shake for Donnie?* If any given action fails to meet Betty's standard of ensuring a fair shake for Donnie and for children, men, and women like him, then we aren't going to do it. It's that simple.

In making a decision to merge, then, The Arc NLC and The Arc Quinebaug had come to the conclusion such a move would better ensure "a fair shake for Donnie" and everybody else who had IDD in Eastern Connecticut. Since both organizations had been affiliated chapters of The Arc of the United States from almost inception, the merger was blessed by a meeting of minds and mission, of purpose.

The Arc's mission and vision differs from nonprofits whose missions charge them to do other (although no less important) things, yet the story of the founding of The Arc itself mirrors the story of all nonprofits in America: Someone saw a need and stepped forward to do something about it. Lillian Mastronunzio, another founding parent, told me that her son Marty's pediatrician mocked her for trying to teach her boy, who also had Down syndrome, to read. "I knew he could read," she said. "And he did learn! He wasn't a great reader, but he could do it. All his life, he loved to read! He would sit there in that chair, and he would read and read and read! It made him so happy."

We all want the best for our families, our communities, ourselves. Being part of a community rooted in the values that gave life to The Arc made it easier to build connectivity and a shared sense of purpose between The Arcs of Quinebaug and New London despite the challenging times in which we found ourselves. The resource integration that mergers require can certainly present challenges for the families an agency serves and for the teams that serve them. Even for like-minded chapters of The Arc, mergers are far from simple and pain-free.

Fortunately, evoking the truths that drove our founding families to launch The Arc movement greatly aided our mutual quest for social change. Indeed, the understanding that we owed it to our founding families not just to survive but to thrive was a common theme that morning in announcing the merger and communicating why The Arc Quinebaug Valley and The Arc NLC's Boards of Directors had decided to merge. It was why we meant it when we told both teams that we were working hard to ensure the impact on their lives and the lives of the people we served would be minimal. Indeed, if anything, we honestly believed that we could promise the merger's results would manifest in positive ways.

We also were able to remind people that a merger between The Arc NLC and Seacorp, Inc., back in 2010 was "good change." It led to improved quality and greater resources for the combined entity, constituents, and team. Like chapters of The Arc, Seacorp had been founded by parents looking for better lives for their children with IDD.

> Both The Arc Quinebaug Valley and The Arc New London County were founded by families more than 66 years ago. We support full inclusion for people with Intellectual and Developmental Disabilities. We've worked together often, including recently, to help you get a higher minimum wage. It makes sense to make that partnership official.
>
> Merging will save critical dollars as it did in prior mergers (Merger Remarks 2019).

Emotion and shock will hang in a room when a merger is announced, as it did in 2019. While mergers are for-profit domains no longer, few nonprofit teams have experienced one. In any nonprofit merger, it's important to reassure teams that the mission to which they have so loyally committed will be carried forth in even stronger and more important ways.

At The Arc ECT, we let people know immediately who the members of the executive team will be. We ask people to work cooperatively. We encourage questions. We tell the team that we believe in them, and we are counting on them: As I stepped forward that morning, surrounded by our new leadership team and board of directors, the message was crafted to reassure. "We know we can count on you to welcome one another to our respective campuses, work cooperatively together and form a new family for a fair and empowering environment—an environment that is positively empowering for people with IDD." We encourage the team to speak to the EAP personnel should anyone feel a need, and then I note that I've walked in their shoes.

> Change can be stressful, but it doesn't have to be. And it's OK to talk about that. We have high expectations and know the future is bright; all the same, if you're struggling with this change we do understand. We continue to encourage people to ask questions and ensure a safe space is provided to do so moving forward.

Next, we invite the team to join us on a journey of excellence. We remind everyone again of shared values: "*We are sister agencies. We will be stronger together! We believe in you. Thank you for working with us to make The Arc ECT the very best agency in the State!*" (Merger Remarks 2019).

Only a small corps of trusted members of the team, on a need-to-know basis, can be brought into the circle of knowledge prior to merger. Teams cannot be left to their own devices to speculate, ruminate, gossip, and spin scenarios devoid of facts. This is critical, as everyone has a good reason why this manager or that one should be brought into the circle of knowledge. The answer is no. Leaking knowledge of a merger can serve only to spread speculation that will drive unfounded fears. The very mission(s) of all entities involved then becomes endangered.

Harsh as it might sound, revealing information prior to official announcements is a serious breach of ethics because the well-being of the many is jeopardized for the short-term curiosity of a few. Team members outside the loop of need-to-know rarely have the maturity or big-picture view to handle secret information responsibly. Look at it this way: People who swim poorly or tentatively endanger even the ablest swimmers.

Upon announcing a merger, we not only encourage people to ask whatever questions they have, we then provide frank answers. All questions are answered with transparency. If we don't know the answer, or if we can't answer the question just yet, we say so.

On the day of the announcement of The Arc Quinebaug/NLC merger, we handed out T-shirts with the new logo and mission: *The Arc Eastern Connecticut—In Partnership for Full Equality.*

At the announcement sites, where shock and curiosity and concern and hope commingled with nervous conversation, we began an honest dialog with the conjoined teams. (You will know when you've set the right tone. Someone in the room will have the courage to ask the question everyone is thinking: "Will we still have jobs? Do I still have a job?")

Since *truth* builds *trust*, we tell the truth. In this case, the truth usually sounds like this: "We believe the answer to that is yes. The outcome is up to you. If you are willing to work hard, work smart—and if you are willing to embrace excellence—there is no reason you will *not* have a job."

Somebody raises a hand. *"Do you ever fire people?"*

Truth. Always truth. "Will every person in this room still have a job in a year's time? Some people might find the journey uncomfortable and opt out. We respect that. Frankly, the agency simply cannot have too much talent. We believe there's a wonderful talent pool here! We want to retain this agency's talent!"

Truth = Trust. I prefer that the conversation become informal at this point: "Let me tell you up front what you can do to enhance your own job security."

Being able to readily produce a list of qualities you value in an employee need not be an exercise born of merger. Indeed, every team member in every organization that truly values excellence deserves to know what habits are valued and rewarded. This is The Arc ECT's list of qualities we seek and value in team members.

Hallmarks of an Excellent Team Member

1. **VALUES.** Puts the health and safety of the agency's program participants FIRST.
2. **VIRTUE.** Tells the truth.
3. **ETHICS.** Stays focused, and helps teammates stay focused, on the agency's mission and/or vision and work. Spreading negative rumors is divisive and cannot be tolerated.
4. **BEHAVIOR.** Opposes bullies and bullying by modeling respectful behavior. Everybody has a bad day now and then, but threatening behaviors are not permitted at The Arc ECT. Turf wars are not permitted, either. People are invited to work in teams, and those who struggle are encouraged to embrace a new way of doing things or move on. The Trust Equation is a great way to model positive behaviors that serve as powerful antidotes against bullying. Remember: Everyone needs a safe place to create.

5. **SKILLS.** Embraces required trainings and/or technologies. In other words, enthusiastically JOINS our journey of excellence.

And more truth. We do let people know:

Mergers happen for a reason. Some people might be reassigned. This partnership is going to be about excellence *and* efficiency. People who keep an open mind and maintain an openness to learning new things and new ways of doing things have absolutely nothing to fear. In fact, we encourage you to talk to team members who have been involved in the prior merger(s) of our organization. Don't ask *us* if you'll be better off. *Ask your colleagues.*

We offer ongoing reinforcement, too: "We mean it when we say that we are always looking for talent." Smart companies and smart leaders build excellent teams. Smart companies and smart leaders do all they can to hang on to excellent employees. In fact, mergers are perfect opportunities for scouting new talent, and The Arc ECT sees every merger as an opportunity to do just that. At The Arc ECT, mergers represent greater opportunity for all.

All of us.

Of course, wherever you go, whether you are doing mergers or not, there will always be a few people who don't want to be on your team. Some folks don't want to be on *any* team.

About 10 years ago, I worked with a man of amazing talent. Geoffrey* walked into my office one day and handed me a couple of music CDs with a knowing wink. He wore a paisley vest, and his blond hair was immaculately coiffed. He ambled about the building like he owned the place ... and, as if he did not have anything particular to do. You wouldn't have needed to be a CEO for five minutes to know that Geoffrey's self-assignment was buddying up to the CEO, and that he'd concluded doing so was more beneficial than accomplishing real work.

As the weeks ground by, Geoffrey moseyed by my office several times daily. Had I'd listened to those CDs? Apologetically, I'd tell him I was getting around to it and, of course—meeting his wink with a big smile—looking forward to it!

One day a friend stopped by on our way to lunch. She picked up one of Geoffrey's CDs from my desk reverently and with a bit of fervor: "I *love* Tuesday's Leap Frog*!"

Feeling like a slacker, I confessed I'd never heard of Tuesday's Leap Frog.

My friend regaled me. Pedigree. Concerts. Contemporaries in the field. I heard a string of household names. "And Tuesday's Leapfrog was better than them all!" she finished in full swoon.

That piqued my interest. Slipping a disk into the console of my Equinox on the way home, I discovered that Tuesday's Leap Frog really was a very good band. Every now and then, even today, when I have my library on shuffle, I'll be driving down the highway and suddenly there's Geoffrey's beautiful, deep baritone. Never mind that the band broke up after the bass player ran off with Geoffrey's wife. For one fame-painted moment, Geoffrey had been a bona-fide star.

To this day, I smile when I remember him picking up a guitar. With flourish, effortlessly, like a butterfly doing what God created it to do, Geoffrey's fingers danced along the strings. His voice, deep and rich as fine chocolate, is something I never tire of hearing.

Geoffrey's multifaceted accounts of the challenges involved in writing the agency newsletter, on the other hand, rivaled Faulkner with their twists, turns and sentence complexities. He was—as you might imagine—more inventive than most in explaining why the effort would be just a bit late this quarter. And a bit later still. "And, yes, oh dear, I fear we've missed this issue entirely!"

Had the agency had the reserves or the will to pay Geoffrey to sit at his desk and write songs all day, picking up his practice guitar and singing out robustly as our resident troubadour, the marriage might have presented, in Dickensian terms, a lesser disparity of mind and purpose. But we were a nonprofit, and we did not have said will or reserves. One day, in a fit of exasperation, I called Geoffrey to my office. Yes, the newsletter (this would be the *next* newsletter as we'd quite missed the last one) was late again.

So many obstacles. So few newsletters. And every explanation regarding the why of it had a hero amid the tale. The hero was, you guessed it, Geoffrey.

"All of these heroics, Geoffrey," I said. "And still no newsletter! If you've done such a good job, then why does the job remain undone?" All Geoffrey's explanations started with "I." Unfortunately, despite his best efforts, again, all involving "I" statements, Geoffrey conceded, still, *we* had no newsletter! *However...."*

Out of patience, I pointed to the door. "Geoffrey," I told him, "when you walk through that door, *me* becomes *we!*"

Geoffrey never did finish the newsletter. The team bailed him out, and they let me know they weren't happy about it. Tuesday's Leap Frog was no more, but the thrill of singing to tens of thousands lived on in Geoffrey's mind. Amid all that applause, there was precious little time for mundane details like creating the agency newsletter. Despite his flair and eloquent prose, to nobody's shock but his own, Geoffrey failed to file an important grant in the ensuing days. This earned him a plaque, a handshake—and an early retirement. He complained at his retirement picnic that I hadn't let him make a speech.

"It was about *you!*" he told me.

So, yes, encouraging employees to explore other options is at times necessary. Only when *me* becomes *we*, can a vocabulary for team building take root. Geoffrey was living proof that charm is not virtue. Even one Geoffrey can create dissonance for an entire team by beating the drum of *me*. After all, the language, the vocabulary, of a team is *we*. It is also the essence of actualized excellence. If employees hold on to *me, my*, and *mine* postmerger—*or the way things used to be* during any kind of important transition—it is time to bring in a facilitator to encourage people to put yesterday behind. EAPs often have skilled industrial psychologists who can help build a cooperative spirit by leading team-building exercises and facilitations and aiding the team in arriving at a shared vocabulary for transformative excellence.

Facilitation really does work.

Sometimes good team members get derailed postmerger by their own poor habits, by their anxieties or by following the lead of a disgruntled troublemaker. Sometimes professional immaturity will impede the progress of a newly promoted member of the team. It's important to coach members at all levels of the organizational chart, especially postmerger or posttransition (*including postpromotion*). Trade organizations and community colleges often offer leadership classes and seminars, and The Arc ECT views investing in the professional growth of team members as an investment in our mission and in excellence itself. At such times, excellent leaders do not look at these things as "costs"; rather, we view them as "investments."

In all cases, it is imperative that leaders are direct when behavioral results falter. Like Franklin's "Get up from your desk" moments, the right phrase often will jar a team member from a less desired behavior to a better one.

Some examples of confronting poor behavior in a constructive but clear manner:

> "If you behave disrespectfully to board members, I can't help you."
> "If you miss the filing deadline, I won't have any good choices."
> "If you enjoy flex time but miss deadlines, you can't work here anymore."

Successful mergers and partnerships require clear boundaries and communication, and so do routine functions and operations. What do you *need* people to do? What behaviors simply are *not* allowed? Then, be clear while finding ways to reward and incentivize the behaviors and virtues the organization needs and wants team members to practice.

The individual desire to advance, succeed, and prosper will spur most teams to greater productivity, satisfaction, and excellence. But the key to transforming individual self-interest into team self-interest lies in developing a transformational vocabulary that will move a team from *me* to *we*:

Talent + Training + Teamwork = Transformative Service and Excellence.

Team members will take note of the message when it is consistent in its delivery. Team members will recognize when leadership practices what it preaches.

The Secrets of Building Transformative and Excellent Service

- **TALENT.** Find talent and reward it in ways that allow you to maintain it, nurture it, and grow it.

- **FACILITATION.** Begin team facilitation immediately upon announcing a merger or significant transition; indeed, introduce facilitation whenever friction builds within *any* existing team. Invest in team relations periodically whenever and wherever needed. Sooner is always better. Remember, investment in a team is an investment in excellence.
- **SATISFACTION.** Invest in team happiness (and intervention). Gift cards, raffles, free pizza, branded t-shirts, branded pens, and mugs and fun tchotchkes fuel even better behavior and results whenever a team moves from a less desired habit to more desirable one. All are investments in excellence.
- **TRAIN.** Find the best trainings, participate in them yourself as appropriate, and secure the resources needed to bring knowledge back to the team. Train and train again. Ensure that learning is never punitive or scary. Do all you can to reassure team members that loyalty and learning will be rewarded with professional satisfaction and opportunity. Tell people directly: "We want to invest in you!" (*And then do it.*)
- **LISTEN.** Keep asking, "How are we doing?" and respond proactively and constructively, in ways that reinforce the team's belief that you really want the truth.
- **FEEDBACK.** Give clear, honest feedback and reinforce the ongoing message that learning is the way to excellence. Reward your producers. Avoid punitive action unless the hallmarks of an excellent employee fail to cultivate results even after coaching; then, act swiftly and deliberately to terminate.

In *Nicomachean Ethics*, Aristotle wrote about *virtue* and how education and experience and a life well-lived inform positive outcomes. "Life seems to be common even to plants, but we are seeking what is peculiar to man" (Aristotle 1941, 942 1097b–30). **Practicing good habits, keeping our word, committing to our best efforts, being sincere and truthful and fair—these are the components of an elevated existence, better friendships, solid citizenship, and stronger communities. Indeed, these are the characteristics of organizations and communities and states and even nations that are genuinely dedicated to advancing the common**

good. When I speak of Aristotelean virtue in America today, I get the impression that America is a nation hungry for a resurgence of virtue.

If you Google virtue, entry after entry will cite *excellence*. It's true that the fruits derived from an ongoing practice of constructive habits surely can be defined as *excellence*. Yet, we sell ourselves short by equating *virtue* to *excellence* without offering a greater context, an Aristotelean one.

Excellence, as Aristotle originally defined it, requires tapping into our better selves when the problem-solving begins. Excellence means making commitments to one another as a team and keeping our promises to one another. Nothing brings about constructive change more readily than a team or a community of human beings, all reinforcing the very best talents and skills each has to offer. Nothing transforms results more so or better than people trusting one another enough to create together.

If all of this is excellence, it once was virtue, and it was a bigger word then, with greater responsibilities implied. When we talk about *11 Secrets of Nonprofit Excellence*, we are talking, in this book, about a greater vision than the modern vernacular generally appropriates.

My friend Martin is a neuroscientist for an international pharmaceutical corporation. Arlean is a small business owner, and Martin is her husband. Over a glass of wine one evening after work, our conversation turned to leadership. We all agreed that one cannot lead without first securing the trust of the team.

Martin said he believes humility in leadership is a critical component of trust-building.

The Wall Street Journal, I told him, had just published an article indicating a new business trend. The newspaper called it "hiring for humility." Studies indicate that humility pairs naturally with honesty. Attributes of humility include sincerity, modesty, fairness, truthfulness, and unpretentiousness (Shellenbarger 2019). All of these are virtues, and they also are building blocks for excellence (nee virtue).

Martin agreed. "When people see you being vulnerable," he said, "they feel safe doing the same. And you have to be humble to be vulnerable."

Leaders don't need to have all the answers. It's important to be honest (humble) when you don't. Acknowledging that you don't know everything, that you as a leader are still learning and growing, requires a degree of vulnerability. It can be very difficult as a leader to demonstrate vulnerability. And yet, enlisting the team to help solve problems with you can build incredible trust.

Not long after becoming chief executive of The Arc NLC, one of those agencies making up what today is The Arc ECT, our primary funder, the State of Connecticut, hit the fiscal crunch anticipated. Just as need spiked, plummeting tax revenues resulting from The Great Recession sparked unprecedented human service funding cuts. Worse, the cuts came on the heels of more than a decade of flat or reduced funding by the state (Phaneuf 2018). Southeastern Connecticut, where The Arc NLC fulfilled the duties of its founding mission, had fared particularly poorly; there, nonprofits had seen human need increase by as much as 66 percent while grants decreased by nearly 25 percent (McMillen 2014).

The Arc NLC was heading into red ink. Belt-tightening would be required. Worse, there was no end in sight. After years of low wages and spotty revenues, employees justifiably wondered why fair compensation was so elusive. They began to lose trust. Working harder and harder for less and less money was not acceptable. Nor should it ever have been.

It was my job to explain why the unhappy state of affairs was likely to trend for the foreseeable future. Department by department, I made the rounds. The message? Things were bad, yes, and now they were going to get worse. In no quarter was the information well received. The mood of the Community Integration Program (CIP) was particularly sour. The CIP team did some of the most difficult work in the agency. The risk of on-the-job injury was great. Behavioral interventions and physical stressors took their toll daily. Turnover in the department was high. The lack of resources only underscored the job's natural physical and psychological demands.

As I stood in the room where most of the agency's heavy lifting got done, it was clear the team was in no mood for grim explanations, even truthful ones. People wanted to hear that they were going to get pay increases, that some measure of fairness lay in store and that it lay ahead fairly soon. They didn't want to listen to anything else.

It dawned on me that I was standing with people who did not know exactly what a recession was, nor did they care. I was standing with hard-working, honest people who were well-trained in food guidelines, life-skills, toileting, abuse, and neglect prevention, First Aid, blood-borne pathogens, and a host of other important proficiencies. Words like "recession" and "the economy" had begun to feel like excuses for their ongoing mistreatment.

The CIP team was tired of people like me in suits explaining that—no matter how hard they worked, or how smart they worked—they were going to get one more kick in the pants. I was standing with people who did not read newspapers or magazines or watch the evening news because they held down multiple jobs and prayed their cars would start in the morning. Many were one paycheck away from homelessness themselves. Working hard all day, every day, pursuing the so-called American Dream, wasn't working for them. They didn't have time to read newspapers or watch television because they left one job and drove straight to another, often seven days a week. And when they weren't at work, they were taking care of children, grandchildren, and even their own parents.

As I stood among my team members, I realized that 30 years of articulation—as a writer, editor, and publisher—didn't make me all that special. My vocabulary was inadequate for my present role. I was humbled. A lifetime of hard work and accomplishment was meaningless in this room. I was new to The Arc. The team didn't know me. They didn't know my reputation. They didn't know who I was or what I had accomplished, and they didn't care.

Why should they? After two decades of hard work and little or no reward, they were burned out, living check to check, feeling suckered.

So, I tried to explain it another way: "Our agency has problems. Our workers' compensation premiums threaten to put us out of business. Our healthcare costs are increasing 30% per year and our state funding is being cut yet again." As an agency, just when it seemed things could not get worse, they had. Not only were people not getting raises (myself included), but I could not even guess when any of us might.

"You sound like a politician," Zelda* shouted.

"We're going to have to pull together," was all I could think of saying. "You need to vote. We need to let our legislators know that none of us can work amid these conditions any longer. We all have to fight for fair funding. Nobody will fight harder than me. But I can't do it alone."

I had never felt a room like this one. My professional toolbox for fixing the mood of the room was proving thin.

Then, Talibah spoke: "How can we help you?"

At first, I thought she was mocking me, being sarcastic. But her tone softened. "I'm serious," she said. "You're new here. And you have all these problems to solve. Is there anything we can do to help?"

Humble? Yes. I felt humbled in that moment. I met her honesty with my own.

"Yes, you sure can help me."

I explained that we needed to manage our costs better, and I really did need the team's help to make that happen. "I want you to have a safety net when you get injured," I told the team. "But we can't afford our injury rates or our insurance costs right now. We have to work safer. We have to work smarter. Look, I'd much rather give the money to you than some insurance company in New Jersey!"

> If you work smarter and reduce your injury rates; if you do what
> we teach you to do in training; if you make healthier choices …
> I will give back to you every dime we save as an incentive! And I
> will work every day for an increase in your wages until you get it.

It wasn't much, but it was all I had.

"Will you really?" asked Bob. "Will you really share the money with us if we manage to save the agency money?"

"I give you my word that I will. But I have to be honest, Bob. It's going to be a while."

Bob nodded.

In a year's time, workers' compensation claims at The Arc NLC dropped by 300 percent. We had realized a thin surplus (worker's compensation insurance rates require a period of good behavior before they will budge), and everyone got a very modest incentive. The mood of the agency rose disproportionately to the reward. People had just gone on too long with too little appreciation. Finally, we had something to celebrate. Together.

In the ensuing years, we further incentivized training and technology. Some of the cash for this investment was realized via savings resulting from mergers. Tech investment funded by merger savings allowed us to run much leaner and smarter. We also emphasized and invested in workplace safety and wellness. Over a three-year period, during a time when other human service agency employees saw flat wages or even wage cuts, The Arc NLC's employees could opt into incentives totaling 2 percent per year over six years, or 6 percent for the duration. This only enhanced our team spirit.

My friend Martin is right. Humility matters. And humility is particularly important for leaders in Human Service nonprofits. Direct support professionals (DSPs) who serve people with IDD—even those who report a love for the job—experience very high levels of burnout. Turnover runs as high as 45 percent industrywide with low wages often necessitating reliance on state-subsidized health care for dependents, SNAP (food stamps) and food-bank supplemented groceries (President's Committee for People with Intellectual Disabilities 2017).

Those of us in human services are social workers, yes, but we are healers and artists and innovators too. We see possibilities where many do not. We live hopefully, and we sow the seeds of which hope itself is made. We see human beings where bullies see sport. And we walk with people with intellectual disabilities, the world's most marginalized people, toward better lives: to independence, to jobs, to life satisfaction and, yes, even to love.

It's a big job, and yet we do it. We do it together—as a team. It's a wonderful, humbling job full of "trust equations" and "good change." Change can be artful. You just need to know how to do it.

The Secrets of Chapter 4

- AUTHENTICY MATTERS. Truth builds trust.
- SHARED VOCABULARY. *We* is the language of a team. Invest in moving your team from *me* to *we*.
- EXCELLENCE IS A FORMULA. Talent + Training + Teamwork = Transformative Service and Excellence.
- VIRTUE MATTERS. Practice good habits. Keep your word. Commit to your best efforts. Be sincere and truthful and fair. The result will be an elevated existence, strong friendships, a more meaningful community experience.

For Discussion

- STRONG TEAMS ARE WINNING TEAMS. What are the strengths of your team? Where does your potential for getting better lie? List three strengths of your team. List three opportunities for getting even better, for achieving excellence.
- CHANGE AS ART. Think about a time when change jarred your life. Why was it so challenging? Can you think of something that might have facilitated your adjustment? Were there any positive outcomes to that change? Looking back, would you do anything differently in adjusting? Why or why not?
- VIRTUE AS A VALUE. What can you do to become a stronger team player? List the ways.

CHAPTER 5

Win! Learn to Love Strategic Planning

Teams often try to avoid strategic planning, while excellent boards of directors tend to be obsessed with it. This creates tension for a CEO who reports to the board but counts on her team to deliver every day.

In my early years of leadership, this tug-of-war affected my own relationship with strategic planning. I dreaded the pressures of a board that wanted yet another round of planning and a team that, despite their talents and strong performance, resisted strategic planning as an interference with their day-to-day tasks, which they enjoyed. Sometimes, senior team leaders resented strategic planning and dismissed it as a pretension of the board of directors—and maybe even a reflection of the board's vanity. I found this disquieting.

But over the years, my perspective matured. If both my board and my team were essential to our mission's success, what wasn't I seeing? I can't say I had a Eureka moment. Very gradually, though, my perspective broadened. What if both the board and the team were right? Where was the bridge between the parallel roads of thought? Wasn't strategic planning a bit of a distraction? And wasn't it—despite the distraction, and perhaps even *because of it*—critical to excellence and long-term success?

It was my job to communicate the value of strategic planning. Maybe I needed to do a better job of communicating to my team why it mattered. How might I help my team fall in love with "what might be?" Maybe, strategic planning needed to be less of a drudge. Maybe it needed to be ... fun? Maybe, we needed music and laughter and ... even ... s'mores....

If strategic planning was fun, I mused, it might well be more productive. It might well lead to more creative results. It might not be the slog the team dreaded. And the results might be dynamic enough to sway the naysayers on the leadership team, folks who themselves were influential with other team members.

Any organization's leadership team is responsible for ensuring that the close-up view of day-to-day operations remains focused. The board has a responsibility to keep the wide angle, or the long-term view, in its sights. A seasoned CEO need not be torn between two matter-of-fact aspects of operational reality. By communicating the value of strategic planning and making the process enjoyable and meaningful, a CEO can walk each side to success. A strategic plan is a map for success, and a good strategic map will lead the team to true excellence by keeping everyone focused, disciplined, and principled in all the ways a nonprofit mission intends.

When I was 17 years old, my brother Melvin* and his friends drove me to Deer Lake, PA, one early Saturday morning. Muhammad Ali was about to fight Larry Holmes, and I was going to get the scoop for my high school newspaper, *The Cub,* and the local newspaper, *The Boyertown Area Times.*

We arrived early in the morning. Rustic log cabins and tall pines dotted the property, which resembled a mountain lodge or hunting camp. Large rocks bore the names of Muhammad Ali's heroes—and a few nemeses: Rocky Marciano, Joe Louis, and Joe Frazier. The training facility and bunk rooms housed coaches, cooks, sparring partners and, of course, while training, Ali himself. It was not unusual for the press or even friends of Ali to drop by. The day we were there, The Spinners were hanging out, yet nobody acted famous. Despite hits like *The Rubberband Man, I'll Be Around,* and *Working My Way Back to You,* the guys in The Spinners laughed and joked around while we all waited for The Champ to finish his daily, three-hour prefight workout.

Everybody cheered as a group of runners crested a small hill. Dancing and dodging and throwing punches from the middle of the group was none other than Muhammad Ali. He jogged over and began chatting with all of us. He saw my notebook and teased that he'd better be careful if a reporter was standing by.

Then he disappeared into a long, low-slung cabin while the rest of us waited. The Spinners continued to amble around. We weren't the only ordinary fans hanging around, either, and I felt some pressure to deliver. Nobody had guaranteed us an audience with The Champ. Hearing from a friend of a friend who had made an inquiry, we were instructed to show up at the boxing camp at a certain time and, if circumstances and, presumably, the fighter's mood and time constraints aligned—then we'd have a few minutes for an interview.

Now that we had arrived, it was clear a lot of people wanted Ali's attention. I fretted that there might not be time for us all. Or maybe he'd choose a private audience with a group other than ours. Heck, I'd rather hang out with the Spinners, too!

My brother's friend Fritz* broke from our group and walked to the other side of the drive to speak quietly with people who worked for Ali. Fritz returned, shrugging. "It's up to the Champ," he said.

Just before breakfast, we were ushered into the cafeteria, a cavernous space filled with tables. Lights were dim. You could feel a room move when Ali entered it. Just then, he walked through a doorway, pausing for a moment—filling the space—as he assessed the room's occupants.

Then, The Champ walked toward us and sat beside me at a table that stretched almost the length of the room. Introductions were made, and Ali asked questions about where I went to school and the names of the newspapers that might publish the story. He talked about his confidence in winning against Holmes. As we chatted, Ali slapped a square of toast onto a plate full of eggs, sunny side up and soft. He pointed to a handful of pills a trainer had put before him on the table and named each vitamin and supplement and explained how it would help him win his upcoming bout.

When Muhammad Ali arrived anyplace, people looked up from what they were doing. When he spoke, only a momentary hesitation between his thoughts and his speech hinted at the damage so many years of boxing had done to the boxer's brain. He was as pretty as he claimed, prettier even, I'd say, and as fast on his feet as his rapid-fire quips and jabs. Ali's tawny-ginger skin glowed; his features and fitness cut a picture in real time.

Muhammad Ali chatted amiably and generously for almost 40 minutes while his handler paced back and forth looking at his watch. Meanwhile, I kept throwing out questions: What was his advice for kids like me? "Tell them to go to college and get some knowledge. Stay there till you're through. If they can make penicillin out of moldy bread, they can sure make something out of you!"

Muhammad Ali proved to be as much of a scholar as an athlete. He recited whole tracts of great books from memory to support his positions on a variety of topics. Through his life, he had clearly committed to informing himself by reading civilization's important books. If he had an opinion about something, he had arrived at it with deliberation and readily ticked off—sometimes at considerable length—the text that had led him to that place.

Somewhere, I still have his autograph and the inscription that Ali, the philosopher–boxer, wrote. **The lesson of this giant of a man sitting with an aspiring cub reporter as if he had nothing better to do will last a lifetime: "Service to others is the rent we pay for our room here on earth"** (Stauffer n.d.).

It was a powerful lesson for a young journalist because it occurred to me that the man sitting beside me was nothing like the man I'd read about. The Ali whom I had just interviewed was not bombastic. He was not proud. Confident, yes, but prideful? No. When he died, decades later, obituary writers would call Muhammad Ali "the most recognized man in the world."

Many of those accounts rightly affirmed his virtues. Quite a few extolled his generosity. But I understood, in a personal way, that he was the kind of man who would give 40 minutes of his time to a teenager who could do him no favors. It was important to Ali that people understood that Islam made sense to him in ways that a religion he saw as oppressive to his people—Christianity—could not. He saw Islam as a religion that recognized service to others as virtue. I came away from my visit with Muhammad Ali with a reverence for having a purpose in life, for taking responsibility for my role in moving the world toward a better place, and for informing myself as I did so.

Muhammad Ali liked to say that he could "float like a butterfly, sting like a bee. The hands can't hit what the eyes can't see." He built a legendary brand with integrity, wit, skill, and good deeds. As much as integrity is key to effective nonprofit and for-profit branding, it is equally critical to transformation, excellence, and strategic planning because that's what safeguards your mission, your ultimate brand. Your mission, in turn, serves your constituents just as it served the ideals of your organization's founders.

Strategic planning requires that we ask ourselves tough questions about where we've been as an organization and where we are going. Integrity sometimes requires that we do the uncomfortable thing, the thing that our mission requires us to do. Sometimes the questions we have to ask ourselves and others require difficult conversations: Does our favorite program, our flagship program, the program everybody loves the most really serve people optimally? *What else does our mission compel us to face, to do, to fix, or to transform?*

In 2014, as The Arc NLC entered its first round of strategic discernment under my leadership, I knew we had several critical questions to explore. Among The Arc ECT's first programs was a popular outreach effort called Community Life and Advocacy (CL & A). Because people with IDD struggle so much for acceptance, CL & A provides valuable socialization for folks with IDD in our region. From dances to Special Olympics to field trips—CL & A was established to provide families caught up in 24/7 care a break, and that happened whenever The Arc picked people up at their homes and provided a fun and safe outing for the morning, for the evening, or for the day. Across the agency and among families, CL & A received high marks. It was a critical and important respite program for the families of the people we served, and a critical community connection for people with IDD themselves.

But as The Arc NLC weathered the storms of the Great Recession, one of them plowed right into the greatly favored and celebrated CL & A. A little at a time, grants for the program began to be reduced and primary funders began begging off. "This is a very worthy program," one longtime charitable donor wrote, "but the community food bank is running out of food. We had to make some difficult choices, and we can't justify funding a social program when people in our community are going hungry."

Was CL & A still relevant? We certainly thought so. Perhaps we were not selling the program as effectively as we once had done. But the prospect of hungry children and families stuck in my mind. Were we really taking food from the mouths of hungry children to host dances and pizza parties for people with IDD? Was that justifiable if the people we served might otherwise have no social outlet for the week, for the month or for months at a time? Studies, after all, consistently prove isolation is devastating to human health and well-being, and that people with IDD are among the most marginalized folks on the planet. Dances versus food nevertheless presented a moment of truth for the agency. *Did we want CL & A to prevail in snagging dollars if it meant that funding CL & A resulted in children going hungry? What about the studies that equated socialization for people with IDD with health and wellness?* These are exactly the dilemmas that strategic planning is intended to solve. And dances versus food was not the only one we faced.

There were, as well, the staggeringly high rates of sex abuse among the IDD community, some studies reporting it in the neighborhood of 80 percent for women and 30 percent for men (Administration for Community Living 2001). Were we being responsible in providing dances and social fodder for people with IDD if we were failing to provide women and men with tools needed to be safe from predators? Would a program that helped the people we serve grapple with the cold realities of sex abuse and domestic violence serve them better than safe, social engagement with one another? Were the needs mutually exclusive?

Another pressing issue was the statistic that told us the numbers of people with IDD who were actively employed had not changed in 20 years. Was providing people with dances helping them become gainfully employed? Did people with IDD require a more focused and integrated socialization platform, one that connected people with IDD to one another as well as provided outlets for networking with community leaders and employers? *Did we need to pivot like Ali, dancing deftly in a new direction as leaders in service delivery?*

If local funders increasingly demanded programs with demonstrated outcomes, how could we even measure the value of a dance for people with IDD? If the food shelf needed dollars and cents or more donations—what was the responsibility of people with IDD to their own community? If people with IDD really were equal, then what were their responsibilities as full, participating members of our community amid the local stressors and needs presented by a worldwide recession? *Should people with IDD be helping to raise money for the local food bank rather than competing with it for funding dollars?*

These are the kinds of questions that drive strategic plans. And these were the questions we asked ourselves during that year-long process of discernment leading up to the new strategic plan's unveiling in 2015—along with a refreshed mission and vision statement.

As the process kicked off in the Fall of 2014, we already had laid important groundwork. We had made the rounds of our founding families and asked what had led them to establish The Arc NLC.

And now, on that September night, despite some grumbling from the team but amid great expectations among the board of directors, the IT folks potted *Camp Town Ladies* to a fade and we all rolled up our sleeves. Because one of The Arc's earliest programs was a summer camp experience for people with IDD, we'd decided to have some fun with strategic planning. To put people at ease and help everyone tap their imaginations, we'd set up a camp theme. Props suggesting trees and tents and outdoor life had been staged around the room where we'd all gathered. Soft drinks and coffee and camp snacks had been laid out. Several small indoor camp stoves were surrounded by marshmallows and melting chocolate in pots and graham crackers. Nothing breaks the ice better than laughter and potato chips and soft drinks … and s'mores.…

Because a strategic planning facilitator's job is to get the ball rolling, ours began with a full review of the agency's mission and vision statement. With help from the people we serve, our advocates, we quickly came to an understanding about some key words the mission needed to convey: "Partnership" and "FULL equality" (emphasis the advocates') were elements the people we serve deemed essential to our mission statement. We began asking ourselves wide-ranging yet grounding, essential, questions: Why had our founding families established our agency? Why were longtime funders finding the goals of one of our favored programs underwhelming? What words would make our mission both more contemporary and more universally accessible? *What would be a fair shake for Donnie?*

Our team and board and advocates anticipated that moving forward we would need to be engaged more in our community. The people we serve emphasized they wanted greater choice and support to live bigger lives in our community.

Customer service was mentioned: Were the CL & A as well as the rest of our core programs, the residential, employment, and day programs, giving the people we served what they wanted? Were they delivering the appropriate outcomes to our funders and, hence, to our community? In some cases, our families told us, the answer was yes. In other ways, they needed more: More flexibility, more support getting loved ones to jobs, and more support in finding quality time to spend with the rest of the family.

Funding, as always, was a big concern. As anticipated, as the hedge fund barons of Fairfield County in the western half of the state felt the punch of the Great Recession, Connecticut's tax revenues began to plunge, and bigger and bigger deficits were getting headlines. Successive rounds of funding cuts kept rolling in. How were we going to thrive in an environment of budget cuts when our state- and federal-funded reimbursement rates for those programs had remained flat or seen cuts in the past 10 years—even while the cost of everything had gone up?

The Arc's Board of Directors challenged themselves as well. How might they better support the agency in its fundraising and development goals? What did strategic leadership look like in the 21st century, and how might we best meet the modern expectation?

When strategic plans work, it's because the messaging is clear, goals are concrete, and the team agrees on the vision and buys into the plan. The strategic plan itself not only articulates a shared vision, it serves also as a blueprint for progress. Compiled in one document, a strategic plan ensures the entire agency is on the same page, and the planning sessions themselves reflect the conclusions of a facilitated and respectful dialog. The sessions offer safe space to voice hopes, dreams, and concerns—even concerns about viability and relevance—both for individual programs and for the very mission and vision of the organization itself.

Among the important questions asked during The Arc ECT's strategic discernment exercises, beyond a reevaluation of existing programs, were those that explored the agency's opportunities for expansion. There was a growing awareness in our community of brain trauma among veterans returning from war in the Middle East. *Should The Arc be doing something for our veterans?*

"What's a fair shake for Donnie?" If The Arc aimed to partner with people living with IDD for equal participation and inclusion in their communities in Eastern Connecticut, the group concluded, then noble

as supporting our veterans would be, doing so presented mission drift for The Arc NLC. Donnie would not have served in the military, and while there likely were things people with IDD could and probably *should* do to support America's veterans, treating battle-induced brain trauma didn't seem to be a fundamental charge of The Arc itself. Besides, a bit of checking on iPhones revealed several agencies in our region were already addressing this need.

As we worked in small groups, we further discussed the needs of the people and families we served and how that had evolved in the last decade. Advocates (people with IDD themselves) and their families were vocal with regard not only to current needs but also to the challenges they believed the future held in store.

The Arc had been founded by families who wanted state-run institutions like Willowbrook and Southbury shuttered so their loved ones could live normal lives, work real jobs, and reside in their own apartments in neighborhoods like yours and mine. But we had not done a great job at finding people jobs in the last 20 years, had we? We had not made a lot of progress in helping people *independently* establish their own homes and lives.

An interesting thing had happened as government shut down its institutions and began funding nonprofits to provide services to people and families dealing with IDD, state by state. Individual U.S. states had begun to fund nonprofits that offered services that looked a lot like the services of those shuttered institutions, that is, the states themselves.

Instead of funding individualized job training to facilitate the sophisticated networking required to land jobs for people stigmatized and marginalized in their communities, states funded employment crews—groups of people with IDD all riding in the same van to the same job, doing cleaning or lawn work—because serving people in groups was much cheaper than serving individual human beings. Instead of funding networked job development so that connected community leaders could work full time at cultivating jobs for people with IDD, jobs to which people with IDD actually aspired, states funded the complex role of job developer at minimum wage or just a bit above that. Entry-level workers with few networking skills and little-to-no personal networks were being charged with supporting people with IDD, people with highly complex challenges, in finding community jobs. No wonder the numbers had remained flat for two decades!

Connecticut, like other states, created regulatory bureaucracies and service models reflective of its own longstanding institutional service models. Where work crews once had functioned in institutional settings, they simply had been moved into communities under the umbrella of private providers, nonprofits like The Arc. The state then charged us with finding jobs for people with IDD in community settings—but offered no real investment to help marginalized people gain the necessary skills required to compete for and keep real jobs.

No investment was made in establishing community networks, the types that the rest of us use, to land real jobs. Worse, when a smattering of jobs was landed here and there, in isolation, well-meaning employers too often discovered the performance of people with IDD was substandard, which reinforced the very stereotypes we were trying to overcome. Tensions between family needs and employer needs (i.e., families needed loved ones to work daytime hours so they too could work; usually, employers struggled to find workers for second shift) were at times acknowledged but never constructively addressed.

If The Arc were to reinvent itself as an agency of the future, it was going to have to adapt and become responsive to what families wanted, what people with IDD wanted and needed, and to find ways to provide the services and outcomes required within the existing structure or convince our funder, the state of Connecticut, to change that structure.

HOW PARADIGM SHIFTS HAPPEN

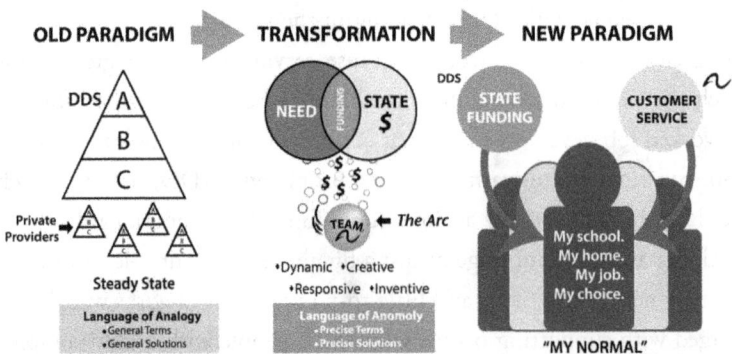

Indeed, The Arc was going to need to embrace the kind of reinvention that nonprofits often resist, but for-profits take in stride. We needed to embrace a paradigm shift: Like Avon, for example, whose founder, David H. McConnell, realized women customers were more interested in the free perfume samples than the books he was selling and thus began a beauty products company; like HP, then Hewlett-Packard, which pivoted from making electrical testing products to home computers, which America's households had begun to demand; and, like Starbucks, which sold espresso makers and coffee beans before establishing coffee shops on street corners because this convenience was demanded by the modern consumer (Nazar 2013). For its part, The Arc was going to have to work with people with IDD to figure out what "My Life" looked like and then take a supportive role in helping people to build it—whatever that entailed.

In human services, those of us providing support for people with IDD had passed around buzzwords like "choice" and "empowerment" for decades. Having spent 30 years in communications, I sometimes wondered if certain words had been deployed for so long as to have lost the real meaning. So, we set about recasting the traditional vocabulary in favor of new terms that would resonate for both the people we served as well as our direct support professionals whose daily interactions had the power to reinforce or undermine personal choice, growth, and independence. Indeed, we set about creating what I call a "Vocabulary for Change."

As we continued our discernment and strategizing throughout 2014, we realized that our agency's foray into reinvention had to happen amid an existing one-size-fits-all service model that had been put, traditionally (by virtue of Connecticut state statutes), rigidly in place—often by legislative fiat. People like to complain about bureaucracy, but the common assumption that bureaucracy does not work is a myth. Take, for example, the Marshall Plan, a $15 billion blueprint for rebuilding Europe after World War II. If you need to build bridges or boats, bureaucracy can be extremely efficient. However, bureaucracy is a system of replication, a means of delivering exactly the same thing in the same way over and over again.

For people with intellectual disability and their families, individual needs and abilities are ill-served by the consistent and repetitive one-size-fits-all offerings of bureaucratic institutions. To really succeed, The Arc was going to have to learn to serve individual needs rather than provide the much cheaper bureaucratic models offered by (and regulated by) Connecticut's Department of Developmental Disabilities. Solutions would need to be inventive and responsive. In short, The Arc was going to have to behave more like a for-profit business than a nonprofit to thrive.

Every nonprofit and for-profit business can reinvent itself. Strategic planning, by its very nature, affords a structure and values-based approach to planful reinvention and transformation. **The CEO needs to own the strategic planning process without taking it over, get input on competent strategic planning facilitators, and take that information back to the board of directors for assessment and decision making. It can be a bit of a dance to keep people focused while not taking over.** I like to sit back during strategic planning and, having supported the board in choosing the best facilitator, let the process work.

An important executive tool, for me, is a small, red French leather diary. During strategic planning and during my regular rounds at the agency, I carry this precious book. In it, I write suggestions, ideas, and big thoughts. A highly engaged team brings forth many excellent ideas, and the diary is particularly useful for this reason. During strategic planning, I record important breakthroughs and team milestones. This guarantees follow-up (by me), and it ensures that big ideas do not get lost. Such a notebook can be an invaluable tool for every CEO.

One of the things I like the most about strategic planning is that it evolves. Our strategic plan of 2015 focused mostly on process. In 2019, when we engaged in a new round of discernment, a full year of asking questions, listening, and organizing what we learned, our constituents emphasized that the new plan called for responsiveness and speed.

Strategic management approaches are meant to evolve over time. Internationally recognized strategy and planning expert Robert M. Grant, currently a professor of Strategic Management at Bocconi University in Milan and visiting professor at Georgetown University in Washington, DC, mapped the evolution of strategic planning over the last 65 years in his book, *Contemporary Strategy Analysis*.

Strategic Planning Trends
Over 65 Years

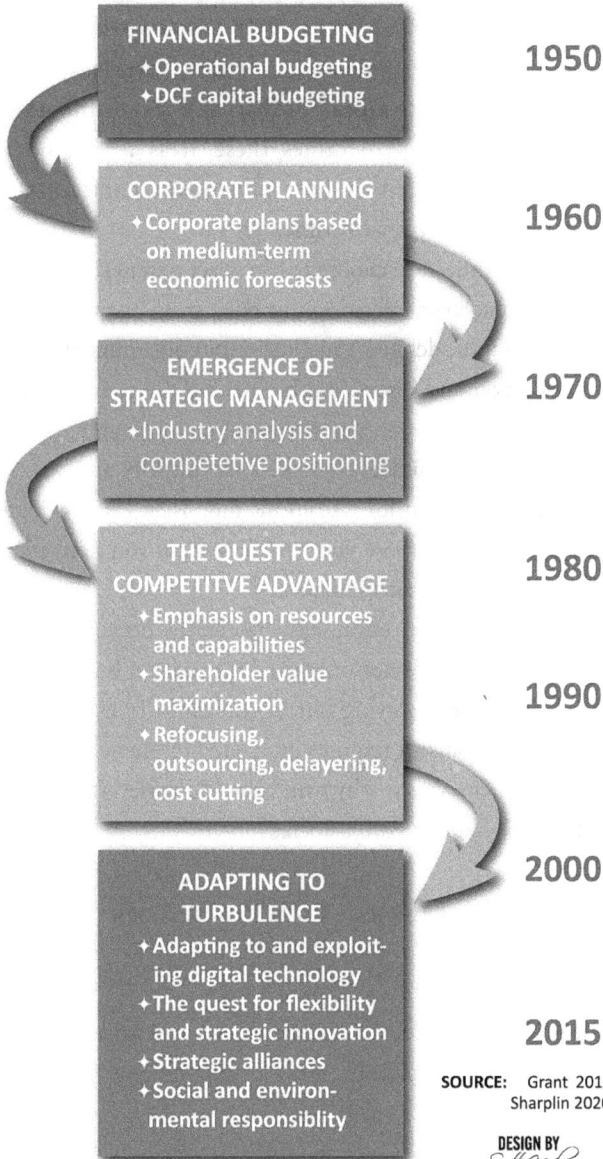

FINANCIAL BUDGETING
+ Operational budgeting
+ DCF capital budgeting

1950

CORPORATE PLANNING
+ Corporate plans based on medium-term economic forecasts

1960

EMERGENCE OF STRATEGIC MANAGEMENT
+ Industry analysis and competetive positioning

1970

THE QUEST FOR COMPETITVE ADVANTAGE
+ Emphasis on resources and capabilities
+ Shareholder value maximization
+ Refocusing, outsourcing, delayering, cost cutting

1980

1990

ADAPTING TO TURBULENCE
+ Adapting to and exploiting digital technology
+ The quest for flexibility and strategic innovation
+ Strategic alliances
+ Social and environmental responsiblity

2000

2015

SOURCE: Grant 2016
Sharplin 2020

DESIGN BY
Scott Kirby

Note how strategic planning trends have grown ever more sophisticated—from simple budgeting to competitive analysis to strategic partnering in order to optimize strategic positioning. One classic strategic planning tool well-suited for the greater complexity of modern enterprises is the **Mckinsey 7S Framework**, which focuses on seven key aspects of operational vision: **Strategy, Structure, Systems, Style, Shared values, Skills, and Staff (Team)**. Why? Because McKinsey rightly identifies these areas as the operational elements of an organization that most influence outcomes, and because these elements must evolve with time.

Should your organization choose not to select a strategic planning facilitator, simply use the chart offered in this book (with adaptations made by the author and a graphic designer) and begin your discernment, an extended period of exploration and discussion, by inviting the team and your constituents and members of your greater community to examine each critical aspect of your programs and operations. First, identify areas of need and areas needing to be targeted for transformation. Then list your opportunities, resources for change (those you have and those you need to acquire), along with action steps for each initiative.

But take note—I favor engaging a facilitator because it allows the CEO to sit back and assess not only the organization but also the transformation process that is playing out in real time. Transformation challenges us so much because it requires integrated implementation *across all operational sectors*. And this is why I find the McKinsey 7S Framework so powerful. It helps leaders to do just that.

The Mckinsey 7S Framework

Strategy

By using mission and vision the organization's objectives become clear. You can find these elements in the strategic planning of an organization.

Structure

How is the organization structured and which hierarchical layers are there.

Systems

Systems are all formal and informal methods of operation, procedures, and communication flows. Soft elements.

Style

Style is all about leadership and management styles.

Shared Values

The standards and values and other forms of ethics within an organization in which vision, corporate culture, and identity are the key elements.

Skills

These concern both the skills of the organization and those of the employees.

Staff (Team)

This soft element is about the employees, their competencies, and job descriptions.

(*In Search of Excellence* 2006).

Note how strategic planning trends have grown ever more sophisticated—from simple budgeting to competitive analysis to strategic partnering in order to optimize strategic positioning. One classic strategic planning tool well-suited for the greater complexity of modern enterprises is the **Mckinsey 7S Framework**, which focuses on seven key aspects of operational vision: **Strategy, Structure, Systems, Style, Shared values, Skills, and Staff (Team)**. Why? Because McKinsey rightly identifies these areas as the operational elements of an organization that most influence outcomes, and because these elements must evolve with time.

My Transformation Plan

STRATEGY		
By using mission and vision, the organization's objectives become clear. You can find these elements in the strategic planning of an organization.		
OPPORTUNITIES	RESOURCES FOR CHANGE	ACTION STEPS

STRUCTURE		
How is the organization structured and which hierarchical layers are there?		
OPPORTUNITIES	RESOURCES FOR CHANGE	ACTION STEPS

SYSTEMS		
Systems are all formal and informal methods of operation, procedures, and communication flows.		
OPPORTUNITIES	RESOURCES FOR CHANGE	ACTION STEPS

STYLE		
Style is all about leadership and management styles.		
OPPORTUNITIES	RESOURCES FOR CHANGE	ACTION STEPS

SHARED VALUES		
The standards and values and other forms of ethics within an organization in which vision, corporate culture, and identity are the key elements.		
OPPORTUNITIES	RESOURCES FOR CHANGE	ACTION STEPS

SKILLS		
These concern both the skills of the organization and those of the employees.		
OPPORTUNITIES	RESOURCES FOR CHANGE	ACTION STEPS

STAFF (TEAM)		
This soft element is about the employees, their competencies, and job descriptions.		
OPPORTUNITIES	RESOURCES FOR CHANGE	ACTION STEPS

Worksheet format ©2022 by Scott Kadey and Kathleen Stauffer

Adapted from T.J. Peters and R.H. Waterman 2006.

To ensure the transformation to excellence occurs in your organization, every aspect of mission, vision, and operations must be fully engaged. This, then, is how The Arc ECT attains, and maintains, transformational excellence ongoing.

What, by the way, became of The Arc's treasured CL & A program as the discernment of 2014 played out? Not surprisingly, people with IDD and their families were critical in helping to reinvent the program. During the discernment discussions, it became clear that dances and Special Olympics were still valued offerings of the longstanding program. CL & A was not needed less; rather, it was needed more—and its scope needed to grow. At the same time, people required a community involvement program that led to greater proficiencies in all areas of life:

- **SELF-ADVOCACY.** Where once leaders at The Arc routinely went to the capital and approached legislative delegates to voice the needs of the people we served, the time had come for people with IDD to speak for themselves. *People wanted to speak for themselves.* Mini classes in self-presentation and human rights testimony would soon become a part of the CL & A programming.
- **VOICES.** Domestic violence prevention and sex abuse prevention needed to become priorities for CL & A. Later that year, leaders at The Arc NLC cross-trained with the region's domestic violence prevention agency, Safe Futures, and support groups for survivors of domestic violence and sex abuse for people with IDD were established. (In the ensuing years, VOICES has become ever more groundbreaking, focusing on being far more preventive in nature. And, due to requests, it now serves men as well as women. But this is where the 2014/2015 discernment and strategic plan began.)
- **VOLUNTEER CORPS.** Networking is a key to success for all of us. Too often, people with IDD are left out of that loop. By establishing a CL & A volunteer corps, people with IDD would be placed squarely into networks with community leaders. The building blocks of careers could be put into place. More important, the volunteer corps became a key component in facilitating an emphasis on ability. There is dignity in helping one another: If you think I am less capable because I am disabled, but I just supported your community event in its successful outcome, then my ability to serve—and my capability to serve—becomes obvious. The CL & A volunteer corps literally turned the community's

preconceived notion of what people with IDD were capable of doing on its head. After one successful fair, the event organizers approached The Arc's CL & A coordinator. "We are sorry," they said, "but we had no idea people with IDD were so talented. Next year, we would like your group to be our lead volunteers. You have changed the way we look at people with IDD!" *(Indeed, the funder that had reduced CL & A funding due to the needs of the food bank reversed course when CL & A volunteers began serving regularly at the food bank. Grant dollars once again were forthcoming and even began to modestly increase.)*

Our discernment process allowed The Arc family to openly discuss what had become a challenging wrinkle in the integrity of our mission and vision. If, as the mission and vision articulate, people with IDD truly are equal, then The Arc's programs need to reflect that. People with IDD are not helpless. Challenged? Yes. Helpless? No. By boldly embracing our mission of equality, reality (and excellence!), The Arc's CL & A programs opened the door to an emerging sense of equality for people with IDD that acknowledges the challenges of disability while demonstrating a capacity for independence—as well as an ability to demonstrate excellence.

The strategic journey toward vocational training and jobs for people with IDD would prove far more complex. A significant portion of The Arc's strategic planning sessions targeted the underwhelming results of jobs training programs for people with IDD, not just within our own agency, but nationwide.

Chapters 7 and 8 will focus on this longstanding challenge and the process of introducing excellence and reinvention into the jobs-training services of The Arc ECT via microenterprise. Here, we will turn to an equally critical aspect of strategic plans that likewise illustrate their inherent value. *Can a strategic plan help a team respond more effectively and rapidly to an international pandemic?* The good news, we discovered at The Arc ECT, is that it sure can.

As valuable as strategic plans can be in good times, they can turn into veritable pay dirt amid a crisis. Once largely immune to market forces, nonprofits can no longer rest on good deeds. To its credit, The Arc's Board of Directors, and the agency's leadership team, had understood that for a full decade by the time the Coronavirus struck in 2020. Fortunately for The Arc ECT, the strategic plan of 2015 had been fully executed and, by 2019, a blueprint had just been written to launch a new one. Newly reconfigured as The Arc ECT postmerger, the agency was well-positioned to face crisis management head-on from a board perspective, a team perspective, from a resource perspective—and from a crisis-management perspective.

The Arc ECT is not alone among nonprofits, by the way, for having quite successfully pivoted during COVID. Indeed, the COVID-19 pandemic, if nothing else, can be credited as the impetus that got many of America's nonprofits moving in real time. As Harvard's Dutch Leonard noted during a nonprofit crisis management workshop for international nonprofit leaders early on during the U.S. pandemic of 2020: "Nonprofits have a reputation for moving slowly. In COVID, nonprofits have discovered the capacity to move faster than before" (Harvard University Business School 2020).

By 2019, in fact, long-term planning and short-term crisis management had merged serendipitously for The Arc ECT although we hadn't consciously realized that yet. I confess, at the time, I did not yet grasp the value that long-term strategic planning might offer amid more immediate crises like pandemics. But The Arc ECT's 2019 strategic plan relied heavily on evolving concepts of quality and innovation. The 2019 plan, then, had a built-in acknowledgment of an ongoing need for rapid innovation while retaining, ensuring, and growing quality. Of particular use, we would learn, were the plan's strategic initiatives.

Five Strategic Initiatives of The Arc Eastern Connecticut

1. **PARTNERSHIPS.** Create and nurture education, housing, employment, and equality through local relationships.
2. **TALENT.** Invest in a diverse and talented workforce.
3. **INFRASTRUCTURE.** Provide welcoming, safe, and functional facilities.

4. **COMMUNITY.** With advocacy, grow donor base, influence, partners, and supporters.
5. **INNOVATION.** Become the "go to" innovator, problem solver, and service collaborator in Connecticut (The Arc Eastern Connecticut 2020).

While I wrote this book, the Coronavirus raged worldwide. Crisis can be a great teacher; survival, a great motivator. At first, we, The Arc's team, wondered if the newly adopted strategic plan should not be put on hold altogether in light of the pandemic.

The Arc's Board members, though, provided the excellent guidance one might hope for from a nonprofit board dedicated to excellent outcomes: Let's not report on strategic planning progress for a few months, they advised. In the meantime, use the plan to point the way to innovative solutions while navigating the crisis at hand.

If The Arc ECT was going to be the "go to" innovator and problem solver among IDD providers during an international pandemic, then the agency's leaders needed to be informed about the virus and its pathology.

With full confidence that I was fulfilling the guidance handed us by the agency's strategic plan, I signed up for webinars hosted by the Centers for Disease Control, seminars sponsored by the New York Academy of Sciences, and the Harvard Crisis Management Workshop as soon as those invitations hit my inbox. Other team members attended briefings by government leaders and community funders. Wherever information might be found, The Arc ECT was there, collecting it from its community partners locally, nationally, and internationally. In other words, we actively sought to nurture partnerships and, where possible, build new ones. In doing so, we ensured that key team members throughout the agency would be well informed and armed with real knowledge of the pathology at hand. This knowledge was then disseminated agencywide, and its sharing in our greater Eastern Connecticut community was encouraged.

From March 2020 through June 2021, The Arc's C-Suite met three times weekly via Zoom for an hour while each member briefed the others, talking about challenges, wins, worries, and more. Group problem-solving prevailed. Emerging crises—such as personal protective equipment (PPE) procurement, sanitizing buildings, staffing support strategies, team messaging needs, and more—consumed the meetings. C-Suite members supported one another with crisis support and constructive feedback and emotional support, too. By July 2021, as the agency and others were asked to begin a gradual reopening in the state of Connecticut, the C-Suite had moved to twice weekly meetings supplemented with in-person interactions amid appropriate social distancing.

Information-sharing remained critical as the pandemic ebbed and flowed, and it became clear that we were engaged in crisis management for the long haul. Through it all, the C-Suite continued to ensure its team members had as much information as possible and that the infrastructure of the agency remained funded and intact. The agency's executives participated in team discussions hosted by The Arc's primary funder, the Connecticut Department of Developmental Services, whose Commissioner Jordan Scheff did a remarkable job of advising and responding to and empowering Connecticut's nonprofit IDD provider community.

At the height of the pandemic, the Connecticut Conferences of Executives of The Arc met every day virtually at 11 a.m. to talk about the latest news on the virus, the most reliable sources of PPE, innovations that were working (and those that were not), as well as other challenges that we, as a group, might help one another to solve. The Arc ECT and its C-Suite executives actively involved ourselves in virtually every one of these Zoom meetings. *As the pandemic unfolded, The Arc ECT began to utilize its strategic plan to implement a plan within a plan.*

When Harvard Business School had launched its virtual Nonprofit Crisis Management Workshop in early Summer 2020 and encouraged 200+ nonprofit CEOs worldwide to participate at no cost, as noted previously, I eagerly signed on with select international colleagues to take advantage of the opportunity.

The similarity of struggles presented by one nonprofit after another, from one nation to another, were uncanny. Despite the wide scope of our missions, service areas, and countries, virtually every leader faced similar challenges and opportunities. We were not that dissimilar in our resourcefulness and problem-solving methodologies either.

Together, we learned that delivering nonprofit services amid an international pandemic might best be aided by the knowledge of what we all had in common. Indeed, none of us was as alone as we had thought.

Markers of Nonprofit Crisis Management Service Delivery

1. **SCOPE.** The crisis was global in scope.
2. **IMPACT.** Its impacts were cascading.
3. **SCALE.** Its scale went beyond anything anyone had to cope with or had seen before.
4. **PRECEDENT.** There was no existing plan to manage what we were dealing with.
5. **FEAR.** People, generally, were afraid.
6. **UNKNOWN.** People, generally, did not know what to expect.

Source: Harvard University Business School 2020.

On June 24 and 25, 2020, for two 90-minute sessions each day, seminar participants collectively explored the magnitude of the international pandemic, the nature of the strategies that might need to be deployed, and the innovations evolving in response to the crisis. The goal was not to help nonprofits survive; rather, the workshop challenged each of us to thrive.

"What do you do when nobody knows what to do?" asked Dutch Leonard, Professor of Public Management at Harvard Business School and the John F. Kennedy School of Government. There was reassurance in hearing our truth spoken aloud: "The definition of crisis leadership is rapid innovation, under stress, in a climate of fear," Leonard said. "This is it folks. You are living crisis leadership" (Harvard University Business School 2020).

As much as strategic planning takes the long view, crisis leadership is all about the quick response. For example, just months prior to COVID-19's sweep across the United States, The Arc ECT's Chief Quality and Operations Officer had ordered additional stores of PPE without knowing whether they ever would be used. Emma* had responded quickly when the scope and scale of the virus began to emerge in the news. I had a sense of it," she later said, "but I didn't have a real sense of it, or I would have ordered a lot more (PPE)" (Stauffer 2020).

Nevertheless, because prior strategic plans (and mergers) had left The Arc well-funded and with a strong development department, additional

PPE supplies—when needed—were readily purchased via cash reserves and grants. Many nonprofits and for-profits ran out of PPE or found themselves without resources to procure it. The Arc ECT never did—because Emma's response had been both immediate and adaptive. Such pivots were, moreover, wholly supported by our existing strategic plan.

The Arc ECT also pivoted from on-site to online service delivery, implementing online delivery innovations within two weeks of Connecticut Governor Ned Lamont's shelter-in-place order on March 20, 2020 (WVIT NBC Connecticut 2020). One huge advantage to having had a strategic plan already in place was that it helped us all to balance the short-term needs of the organization against the long-term needs (Harvard University Business School 2020). Because The Arc ECT had made a commitment to provide concierge services in its 2019 strategic plan, pivoting to meet the needs of families and people with IDD for in-home, online service delivery was matter of fact. I lost no sleep making firm decisions about matters for which the strategic plan had already provided an imprimatur.

Because The Arc ECT also had committed to concierge services for employees to aid in team well-being and retention, rolling out a host of internal communications, hazard pay incentives and podcasts and videos of encouragement for the team agencywide posed no dilemmas either. Making quick decisions to invest in services and team welfare during the COVID-19 pandemic was the one thing, amid what often felt like an impossible situation, that was not too difficult. I was working from a board-approved strategic plan handing me full permission to put the people we served and the people who served them first in line for agency supports and incentives and resources.

Prizes for staying in touch via e-mail, weekly memos that included recipes for stretching budgets and invitations for team members to send personal e-mails telling us how they and their families were doing became bonding rituals among The Arc ECT family. **Five podcasts recorded to inform our families and our team members (approximately 3,000 people) about COVID-19 garnered more than 30,000 views. Clearly, Eastern Connecticut had come to view The Arc ECT as a trusted source of reliable information about the virus in an environment where "truth" had become a politically volatile concept.**

And the invaluable investment in **technological infrastructure** that The Arc ECT had made over a 10-year period (some $3.6 million) paid off exponentially. Technology investment (including a five-person IT staff) proved critical in facilitating the pivot from in-person to online services. Precisely because strategic planning work in the early 2000s, long before I was a part of The Arc team, had called for technological investment of a caliber the board and the team believed necessary for a nonprofit in the 21st century, The Arc ECT was able to respond effectively and immediately to an international crisis unfathomable in the decade that the commitment and plan had been made.

A strategic plan becomes essential during crisis management because it grounds decision making and marries it to a greater vision. At a time when nobody has a lot of time to think, "What's next," the blueprint of a strategic plan serves as a life raft. Even a well-run for-profit or nonprofit will be challenged to its core from time to time. The answers for successfully navigating a crisis of the magnitude of COVID-19, according to Harvard, lie in *process*.

How to Answer: "What's Next?" With Your Strategic Plan

1. **PROCESS.** When you don't have preexisting answers, the answers to the questions emerging lie in process.
2. **ELEMENTS OF PROCESS.** What are they?
   - *Structure.* Look at events as a whole; make sure nothing slips through the cracks. Be honest. Give people hope. Give people empathy.
   - *Who's on your bus?* Make sure you have people on board who understand the internal environment as well as those who understand the external environment. Keep people focused. Reconfigure structure and team members as needed.
   - *Nature of the problem-solving process.* Establish goals and values. Understand the situation. Create options. Predict outcomes. Choose the best approach. Execute. Loop back. Adjust.

Source: Harvard University Business School 2020.

Nothing begs for excellence in leadership more than a crisis. As The Arc ECT weathered the challenges that COVID-19 presented in the areas of health, safety, staffing, and technology, a stronger, more resilient agency began to emerge.

As the Summer of 2020 progressed and the C-Suite was able to consider once again reporting on the progress of the strategic plan, we realized that many, many of the goals laid out in that plan already were being achieved daily. Given the need to innovate, adjust and keep going amid the rapid decision making that crisis management requires, nothing grounds a team better than having already put into place a strategic blueprint for transformation, excellence, and change. Amid crisis, strategic plans become lifelines.

The Secrets of Chapter 5

- NONPROFITS MUST PIVOT. To attain excellence, responsiveness to community needs must be inventive and rapidly adaptive. In this respect, nonprofits have to learn to behave more like for-profit businesses.
- CRITICAL APPLICATIONS. As the pandemic unfolded, The Arc ECT utilized its strategic plan to implement a plan within a plan. A well-crafted strategic plan provides a strong platform for crisis management and pivoting should crisis arise. Nonprofits need to embrace long-term planning consistently and ongoing if they are to competently face the pivots required in the face of life's inevitable, unplanned challenges and unexpected events.

For Discussion

- OPPORTUNITY. In what ways has your organization succeeded in being more like a for-profit than a nonprofit? Where do you see opportunities to do more of it?
- STRATEGIC PLANNING. Have you learned to love it? How will you involve your team in brainstorming and

problem-solving and identifying opportunities? Do you see strategic planning's value to a nonprofit? How might you persuade your team to embrace it? What is the price of inaction? In what ways did The Arc implement a plan within a plan, and what did you learn from its pivoting?

CHAPTER 6

Why Planning for Crisis Is Plan A

When I was first named a corporate division president back in 2005, the CEO who promoted me—a former military man—took me aside one day. "Kathleen," he said, "the team needs to know where you are leading them. If they know where you are going, they will follow. But if they are confused, they will be afraid."

Strategic planning is one of the most sophisticated and critical exercises any organization undertakes. Transformative excellence cannot be attained without an excellent strategic plan. A strategic plan not only lets your team know where you're leading them but it also outlines what you expect from your team. A strategic plan is what I call *a living document*, a dynamic plan moving an organization purposefully and *mindfully* from the past to the future.

Strategic plans are a compass for all team members in an organization. The Arc ECT's Board of Directors feel passionately about strategic planning, and my annual evaluations essentially measure whether we have a good plan and whether we are making it happen. Strategic plans are not so much about change as they are about constructive progress toward excellence, about transformation, because there can be no constructive progress, no excellent achievement, without transformation.

What are the elements of change? For transformation to happen, teams need to be given three things:

Three Secrets for Getting Teams to Embrace Change

1. **INFORMATION.** The team needs to be informed about the scope of what needs to be done and why it's important.
2. **ENGAGEMENT.** The team needs to be involved in creating the plan so there is clarity regarding the why of the processes necessary to

achieve established goals and even the why of the goals themselves. *The team needs to feel it is their plan, not the CEO's plan or even the board's plan. They need to feel empowered to strategize so they will learn to love strategic planning too—or at least develop a practical appreciation for it.*

3. **ACCOUNTABILITY.** Leaders need to be accountable to their constituents and their teams (International City/County Management Association 2005). Remember, once a team knows you will listen to their input and feedback, once a team knows where you are leading them, they will offer input constructively and follow purposefully.

In December 2019, The Arc ECT's Chief Operations and Quality Officer was keeping tabs on her son as he made his way through Southeast Asia. An admitted helicopter mom, Emma followed Elvin's* travels as he worked his way through an internship post college. Increasingly, as the month of December played out, Emma was hearing about an exotic, dangerous, heretofore unknown virus.

Emma grew terrified that her rail-thin, freckled son with his red shock of hair was going to fall victim to a strange malady called the Coronavirus. She began to google "Coronavirus" incessantly.

Sitting at her desk one day, googling, Emma had a horrible thought. What if the Coronavirus traveled to America? The Arc ECT serves close to 1,000 people and all are vulnerable, many physically so. Given what she was reading about the virus's ability to spread, Emma's thoughts flew to The Arc's 22 group homes where 93 people with IDD lived. *How would The Arc keep everyone safe? How would the team avoid transmitting the virus to residents? If residents were to contract this thing called a Coronavirus, how would The Arc protect its direct professional support team from getting sick even as they supported others, toileting, shopping, imparting job training, life skills, and more?*

Emma began to research all the ways the Coronavirus was known to spread. She researched the probability that the virus would, in fact, infect America. Everybody was saying that was unlikely. But Emma's instincts were on full alert. Even after Elvin returned safely to the States, Emma continued to follow the virus. As January 2020 arrived with news seeming ever grimmer, Emma—as previously noted—advised the agency to take a calculated risk. She sought and received my permission to buy PPE. We stocked up on N95 masks, which Emma had read were the recommended front-line protection against a virus now more specifically called COVID-19. She stocked up on generic surgical masks, too. Emma bought Lysol. She bought gallons of hand-sanitizer. She bought thousands of surgical gloves.

By the time the Coronavirus hit America, Emma had stockpiled enough PPE to ensure that, should infection strike, The Arc ECT could keep everyone safe for six weeks. And when the virus did hit American shores, as The Arc began using up that PPE in staggering volumes, even as PPE grew ever more difficult to obtain, Emma just kept buying it. Throughout the pandemic, thanks to Emma's foresight and local community funders, The Arc ECT never had fewer than six weeks' worth of PPE on hand.

While other nonprofit human service agencies were learning what PPE was and why it was needed during the Coronavirus outbreak, The Arc ECT was surveying families and team members to ensure they felt supported, protected, and safe. The Arc ECT was taking team members' temperatures and conducting health assessments at each group home's door (yes, Emma had purchased plenty of thermometers, too), with nursing protocols firmly in place to keep everyone alert to symptoms of COVID-19.

Having launched its second strategic plan in seven years, The Arc ECT was able to pivot with the virus. Stress levels ran high, executives lost sleep, families felt frazzled, and the agency scrambled (and sometimes struggled) to transition from traditional to online services.

The Arc found a way to regularly feed nearly 100 group home residents, often in partnership with local restaurants, food distributors, and grocers. A full complement of internal and external communications was rolled out to keep everyone connected. Guiding all of this was the strategic plan created over a one-year period of discernment the year before and launched only months prior to the pandemic. Input for the plan had come from everyone, from the people The Arc served, their families, direct support professionals, mid-level leaders, deputies, the C-Suite, community partners and the board of directors themselves. Our planning for a crisis as Plan A was paying off, and the team moved the plan, our plan, forward despite unprecedented fears and obstacles.

This is what had sparked Emma's quest for PPE. Her team trusted her to make life-saving decisions every day. She was not about to let them down. And because a well-run agency, *an excellent and strategic agency*, has ample resources and reserves, stockpiling that first batch of PPE, and successive orders as well, was not as problematic for The Arc ECT as it proved to be for so many for-profits and nonprofits nationwide.

Strategic plans help organizations grapple with big questions and provide guidance for working out details. Strategy and process are important because such methodologies walk us through the decision making of plan-building even when, as The Arc's board acknowledged in 2009, the answers to the challenges at hand are not fully known. Some business analysts, for example, questioned the wisdom of launching Disney Cruise Lines in the 1990s without a casino option. But Disney had approached the question strategically.

> The mission of the Walt Disney company is to entertain, inform and inspire people around the globe through the power of unparalleled storytelling, reflecting the iconic brands, creative minds and innovative technologies that make ours the world's premier entertainment company. (The Walt Disney Company n.d.)

If Disney is the place Where Dreams Come True, then how might gambling entertain, inform, and inspire those dreams? On land, the "Disney Difference" means that every child gets the best ride of his or her life at any given time (early in the day or, more important, late in the day) on any given day, in any given theme park. "The Disney Difference," be it on land in or at sea, offers an experience of excellence for every member of every family that engages with each ship, park, or ride.

For The Disney Difference to prevail, fun for the whole family must be the result. The perspective, for Disney then, was that gambling is an adult experience. Therefore, gambling falls outside the scope of what Disney will do (The Walt Disney Company 2013). Simply put, if mommy or daddy loses the house on a Disney cruise, it won't be the best ride of anybody's life.

If The Arc ECT's strategic plan requires that every person it serves and every team member it employs enjoys concierge support, then PPE surely constitutes a priority whether the world is roiling—pandemic or not. When The Arc ECT, then The Arc NLC, embarked upon its first strategic plan under my leadership in 2014, I understood that the board of directors intended for us to answer the questions it had set forth in launching its search for a chief executive: *What does our future look like? Should we be large or small? What will it take to navigate the challenges of the future? What lies ahead?* (Stauffer 2019).

These are precisely the kinds of questions a strategic plan answers.

Again, hiring the right strategic planning facilitator is key to achieving excellence with any strategic plan. Most community foundations can make recommendations for talented strategic planning professionals in your geographic area. Sometimes community funders such as banks also sponsor programs that provide references for strategic planning facilitation, board development, and other long-term needs such as capital campaigns. You might get recommendations too from nonprofit organizations in your area that have their own act together, organizations that are guided by a greater, deliberate plan—a strategic plan.

Facilitators, as noted, allow you (and your team) to have your hands free, so-to-speak, to focus on the hard work of discernment, deep thinking, and discussion that happens during great strategic planning sessions; therefore, again, an outside facilitator is advisable. Providing a framework for discussion, note-taking and summarization is best done by a neutral third party—the strategic planning facilitator.

Nonprofits might survive, but they will not thrive without a solid strategic plan. As your agency or organization rolls into strategic discernment, a talented facilitator will help your team begin the serious business of sketching out parameters and setting the stage for these important discussions and for the plan itself. Every excellent strategic plan requires certain points of integrity if excellence is to result.

The Four Secrets of Strategic Planning Excellence

1. **KEEP IT SHORT.** Mission and Vision statements should be brief, and too often they are not. No matter what, insist that the facilitator lead your team in crafting concise, clear statements that everyone in the organization can memorize. Your mission statement is your

compass, your North Star—and everyone else's, too. It's a universal joke among nonprofits that mission statements are written, put on a shelf, and forgotten. Dry, wordy, Mission, and Vision statements won't inspire people to make them happen.

This is one reason teams so often resist strategic planning. Genuinely busy people want to get their work done, invest their efforts in making a difference. Too many team members have been involved in plans that came to nothing. People get their hopes up, as we all did with R. Bud Whipple. Don't disappoint them.

2. **BE INCLUSIVE.** Buy-in is critical because no team will buy into a plan that they've had no hand in writing, and we've already demonstrated that teams are smarter than individuals—the more diverse, the better. Include as many people as practical. Keeping in mind Scharmer's advice, the inner condition of leadership must be such that leaders facilitate an environment for thinking big thoughts, an environment conducive to creativity, and a safe space for everyone to speak up and share. Leadership, and especially the board of directors, needs to provide the proper conditions for strategic planning work sessions to bear fruit.

3. **BE DYNAMIC.** Teams often find strategic planning boring precisely because it so often is done in boring fashion. Boring strategic planning work sessions lead to mediocre strategic plans. Involve the whole team, the community, participants and their families, agency leaders, and the agency's board of directors. Whenever and wherever possible, introduce elements of fun to strategic planning. Use colorful markers. Allow people to paste things here and there and brainstorm and draw pictures and move about the room. Involve music, fun, food, and exercises that help people to get to know one another. Ensure an environment that aids in building trust so team members will feel comfortable taking brainstorming risks with one another.

4. **BE FLEXIBLE.** Plan for a crisis. Build "what ifs" into your process. This encourages team members to think creatively, and it trains a team to anticipate obstacles and think nimbly. "What if people with IDD stop wanting to live in group homes?" is a good example of a what-if. Where once it was unthinkable that people with IDD would want to live in their own apartments (or could do so safely!), this is the new normal for most young people with IDD graduating from high school

or college. Like other young adults, independence and leaving the nest is an increasingly common expectation; yet it once was thought unattainable! What-ifs need to contain an element of something people might never expect will happen. As we all know, the unexpected happens all the time—and that's often a good thing in the long run. In the meantime, chaos and panic can ensue, but if we have a strong strategic plan, then that plan will guide us through the turbulence.

The Arc ECT's team in 2014 began its strategic planning process by conducting a listening tour with our founding families. This is how we had learned that all Betty Demicco had wanted was "a fair shake for Donnie." Here, then, is where we began, and how we determined The Arc NLC's Question Zero, the question Dutch Leonard at Harvard University Business School defines as, "*What, exactly, are we trying to accomplish* (Leonard 2018)?"

Critical to the strategic planning process for The Arc ECT were the people we serve, whom we call advocates, and their families. We invited the advocates and their families to the table by asking, as previously mentioned: *What do you need for a better life? Are the services we provide the services you want?* Next, we invited every person on the team to write on a piece of paper the answer to this question: *I come to work every day because....*

Team members grew emotional talking about how much what they did every day meant to them. People who wanted to do so took turns reading aloud their answers to why they came to work each day.

Prior to the session, I had read privately through everyone's responses. The numbers of team members who said they worked at The Arc NLC because they believed it was their job to support a person with IDD in living the best life *of his or her choosing* averaged about 25 percent. As I read, I grew increasingly pleased. I was not too worried that we lacked the courage necessary for transformation. Studies put the Tipping Point for social change at 25 percent (University of Pennsylvania n.d.). *From what I was reading, we really did possess the capacity to bring about the organizational change that the people we served and our board of directors desired!*

We've discussed the psychological gap, the poverty of expectation, that results from institutionalization and marginalization. Geraldo Rivera, having blown the whistle on Willowbrook, talked about the outrage and indignity of treating human beings in assembly-line fashion.

So, we were doing a lot more than creating a strategic plan at The Arc NLC in 2014. Institutional models of service for people with IDD that focused on helplessness and a one-size-fits-all response were what states were funding and what a lot of our team members were used to doing. Our advocates and families were telling us they wanted real lives and meaningful community involvement. That we possessed the capacity for change, philosophically, among our direct support professionals was critical. It meant we were poised for real social change, for a true organizational culture shift, to build that team and resources for the future that the board of directors had set out to create. It meant we had the building blocks for excellence in our grasp.

Too often, the poverty of institutional thinking sets up providers who serve people with IDD—and people with IDD themselves—for dissatisfaction or downright failure. If we say we believe that people with IDD have the right to self-determination, but we actually work with people who have IDD because we think doing so makes us heroes, then we really are not working from a standpoint of human equality.

In 2014, as we headed into our first period of strategic planning discernment, we at The Arc NLC wanted our advocates, the people with IDD whom we serve, to do much more than weigh in on the mission and vision of the agency. We knew that we didn't want a traditional mission and vision statement any longer because *we wanted each advocate's mission and vision for his or her life reflected in the mission and vision statements. We wanted to ensure that each person we served could hold us to our promise and provide critical feedback on whether we were supporting people in such a way that "My Life" would become a reality for each one.*

After the initial kick-off session, we met agencywide in small groups on a monthly or bi-monthly basis. The client representative on The Arc NLC's Board of Directors routinely moved back and forth from our advocates, the people whom we serve, and their families to our board and our team to let us know what people wanted and how people felt about the plan's progress. The Arc NLC's client representative served as an active and critical member of the mission and vision's wordsmithing team:

*As noted previously, the advocates were adamant that the words **Partnership** and **FULL equality** had to be a part of the mission statement. Here is what we all came up with:*

OUR VISION FOR PEOPLE LIVING WITH DISABILITY

Equality of opportunity, equality choice

OUR VISION FOR OUR ORGANIZATION

The Arc ECT will be eastern Connecticut's leader in partnering and advocating for equality of opportunity and equality of choice.

OUR MISSION—In Partnership for Full Equality

To PARTNER with people living with intellectual and developmental disability for EQUAL participation and inclusion in the communities of Eastern Connecticut.

Our Completed Strategic Plan Summary Looked Like This

The Arc.
Eastern Connecticut

STRATEGIC PLAN 2020-2023

PARTNERSHIP
FOR FULL
EQUALITY

OUR VISION FOR PEOPLE LIVING WITH DISABILITY
Equality of opportunity, equality of choice

OUR VISION FOR OUR ORGANIZATION
The Arc Eastern Connecticut will be eastern Connecticut's leader in partnering and advocating for equality of opportunity and equality of choice

OUR MISSION IN PARTNERSHIP FOR FULL EQUALITY
To PARTNER with people living with intellectual and developmental disability for EQUAL participation and inclusion in the communities of eastern Connecticut

OPERATING PRINCIPLES

1. **Civil Rights**: We partner with people living with disability to promote their voice and champion their perspective.

2. **Community**: We facilitate the development of natural relationships to connect people with their communities.

3. **Innovation**: We continuously break new ground in providing a menu of service options and improve how we operate our organization, to bring about meaningful change for the future.

4. **Family**: We encourage and facilitate family education and engagement as fundamental to helping people living with disability achieve positive outcomes.

5. **Leadership**: We model choice in everything we do.

6. **Change**: We will change our community by modeling and raising awareness of our mission.

OUR VALUES

1. **Person-centered**: We respect and respond to individual choices as the guiding force in the lives of people living with intellectual and developmental disability.

2. **Dedication**: Organizationally and individually we are dedicated to people living with disability who place their trust in us to provide quality individualized, self-directed supports.

3. **Integrity**: We uphold the highest ethical standards in how we treat people living with disability and in how we operate our organization.

4. **Stewardship**: We are fully committed to protecting and maximizing the return on the resources available to us and to embracing the highest standards of accountability.

STRATEGIC INITIATIVE 1

CREATE AND NURTURE STRONG PARTNERSHIPS

The Arc Eastern Connecticut values a person-centered approach in all that we do. We are committed to strengthening and advancing relationships through concierge-style services to customers and team members alike, offering education, advocacy, community partnerships and collaborations. We are committed to having a customer base and team reflective of our community.

STRATEGIC INITIATIVE 2

INVEST IN A DIVERSE & TALENTED WORKFORCE

The Arc Eastern Connecticut is committed to building a workforce that invests in its most valuable resource, its people (person-centered.) We are committed to providing the team with training, personal and professional development, access to technology and fair and consistent hiring, evaluation and retention processes.

STRATEGIC INITIATIVE 3

INFRASTRUCTURE

The Arc Eastern Connecticut will provide welcoming, safe and functional facilities. It is our priority to consistently align facility needs with resources to ensure proper use and growth.

STRATEGIC INITIATIVE 4

COMMUNITY ENGAGEMENT

The Arc Eastern Connecticut values its advocates, partners, and supporters. We believe we are stronger together. We are committed to growing our donor base, developing planned giving and setting annual fundraising goals.

STRATEGIC INITIATIVE 5

INNOVATION

The Arc Eastern Connecticut holds innovation, creativity and optimization in high regard. As we grow, we are committed to providing plans that make The Arc Eastern Connecticut the "go to" innovator, problem solver, and service collaborator for Connecticut.

A proper mission and vision drive a strategic plan. Once these principles are in place, and once an organization's constituents and its team agree that these are, indeed, the correct operational concepts for creating, reframing and/or building upon, and once the board of directors has ratified the plan, then each department of The Arc is free to work with the people it serves to *re-envision* services via the framework, in accordance with each person's dreams. These dreams, summarized, in turn become action steps within the corresponding strategic initiatives. (Please see accompanying strategic plan illustration.)

It was The Arc ECT's day program team that first came up with a term that is commonly used by all of us now. But when introduced, it was cutting edge. *Concierge supports*, small group outings with people being polled on what activities they wanted to do, with folks opting into the activities of the day when they arrived at The Arc in the morning, became a new standard. Employment program participants wanted real jobs, so we made plans to launch microbusinesses to provide paying vocational opportunities for people to train in their areas of interest. (Ideally, these business revenues—our board counseled—would likewise contribute to a more stable funding stream for the agency, especially in uncertain times.)

It would not be until four years later, though, following a discernment and strategic planning exercise sparked by The Arc NLC/Quinebaug merger, that the concept of implementing a targeted *concierge response for team members themselves* took root. It was during these strategic discussions that The Arc ECT's Board of Directors and leadership team and DSPs and advocates and families realized concierge services were not just for the people we serve, but for the people who serve—our direct support professionals and our entire team.

Among their greatest obstacles to inclusion and equality, advocates and families alike agreed, was turnover among support professionals. Operating from the principle that people cannot empower unless they themselves are empowered, The Arc ECT made a commitment to be more than a model agency serving people with IDD. We also would be a model employer. In its postmerger strategic plan, The Arc ECT, newly born of the merger between The Arcs of Quinebaug and New London County, pledged not only to invest in quality services but also to consciously invest in the team that would be providing them. It wasn't going to be easy, given the funding trends in Connecticut and in states nationwide. It wasn't going to be easy to do during the pandemic that none of us yet knew lay ahead, nor in the aftermath of the new normal. But that's what a strategic plan is for—weathering storms, present and future, with an intentional flare for excellence.

The Secrets of Chapter 6

- FOUR DUTIES OF A CEO. Plan for a crisis. Anticipate trouble, prevent it or pivot to opportunity. Build a great team. Ensure the team has the resources it needs. Set the tone for the organization.

- THREE ELEMENTS OF CHANGE. Teams need information, engagement, and trust if they are going to effect change.
- THREE SECRETS OF STRATEGIC PLANNING. Keep it short; be inclusive; be dynamic.

For Discussion

- ATMOSPHERE. What is the tone of your organization? Are people stuck or energized when they run into unexpected challenges? Do your employees work as a team? Do they have the resources they need? Is change in order? What kind of change? What will it take for the change you need to happen?
- TRANSFORMATION. Do people in your organization believe they have the information they need to do an excellent job? Are they invested in your mission? Do they trust the leaders in your organization?
- ACTION. What is your plan to achieve your goals? Is this a team-driven plan? How can it become the work of all concerned? Is it exciting? If not, what must occur to get people to embrace it with enthusiasm?

CHAPTER 7

Mentors Are Mandatory!

Do you deal with the problem you have ... or the problem you want? Successful CEOs and successful boards of directors must have the courage to face facts.

Prior to the merger with The Arc Quinebaug Valley, with the launch of its 2015 strategic plan, The Arc NLC had committed to tackling various challenges whose roots had been years in the making. Among the most vexing of these was reinventing employment services for people with IDD. Why had rates of employment remained flat for two decades nationwide?

The Arc NLC did have a right to be proud of one aspect of its existing employment training platform: Many other service providers had responded to their charge by handing people with IDD jobs in house-run "training" enterprises called sheltered workshops, busy-work operations that paid subminimum wage for unskilled, repetitive tasks. Some of these "jobs" were productive vis-à-vis the outside world (gluing greeting cards together, for example) but some were not (putting items from one box to another and then repeating the exercise over and over).

The Arc NLC and its board of directors had resolved years before I was hired that it would pay minimum wage or more to people with IDD whom the agency served in its training enterprises, and the agency would only place people with IDD into community jobs that paid minimum wage or higher. (Taking a short cut to placing people with IDD into jobs by allowing a community employer to pay subminimum wage likewise was unacceptable).

The decision was mission-driven, and it lay at the heart of the agency's commitment to honor the dignity of people with IDD. The integrity of this resolution impressed me when I interviewed for the CEO job, and it was a significant factor in my interest in the job. *If we really believed people with IDD were equal and capable of accomplishing real work, why would we pay folks subminimum wages? Why would anyone?*

While it might shock the public, even today many agencies charged with training people with IDD for jobs continue to pay subminimum wages. The same agencies then place the people with IDD whom they've trained into community jobs with employers who also pay subminimum wage. Some providers aggressively lobby to continue doing so even while claiming a belief in equality and equal treatment for people with IDD. Fortunately, this sentiment has begun to shift in recent years, and federal law is tightening around the practice. Nevertheless, paying subminimum wages continues, even now.

That said, it's one thing to commit to doing the right thing, quite another to make it happen. The charge of figuring out how to solve this conundrum was ours. Fiscal analysis revealed that if, as resolved, we continued to pay minimum wage in vocational programs that didn't generate revenues sufficient to pay those wages, and if we continued to grow our employment program, the agency would fall into a $300,000+ annual deficit within three years. We'd be out of business in five.

There was another troubling aspect to our employment training services model in spite of our good intentions: When The Arc cleaning crew, in a vocational training exercise intended to prepare people for cleaning jobs in community businesses, "cleaned" my office—they really didn't. We were so committed to loving people with IDD, so in love with the *notion* that everybody was equal, that we didn't actually train people with IDD to do real jobs by helping folks to develop real skills. But we still paid everybody minimum wage!

As I looked at an agency bottom line rapidly disintegrating due, in part, to payment of minimum wages for which there were insufficient supporting revenues, I realized we didn't have a lot of time. Had we been successfully training people for real jobs, and placing people in jobs around the region, that would have been one thing. In that case, my job would have been simpler—cutting costs and/or growing revenues to ensure positive revenue flows. (*The problem I wanted might have been that one!*)

The problem I had was considerably more challenging. It required moving an entire service platform, employment services for people with

IDD, from an ineffective and unprofitable structure to an effective and profitable one. To our knowledge, nobody had done that yet. *How best to transform the culture of The Arc from an enabling environment to an entre-preneurial, dynamic model? Before The Arc could successfully prepare people with IDD for jobs, we needed to train the trainers too.*

Here again, clarity about what needed to happen was key: A lot of agencies clearly had solved the problem they wanted by simply adjusting the rate of pay below the minimum wage—far simpler than developing real training programs for capable yet complicated people. What happens when you pay less and expect less? *You get less!*

The Arc ECT already supported two cleaning crews, one that quite capably performed standard cleaning tasks at various local businesses and one that cleaned our own buildings. While the crew working outside the building had a core group of cleaners with IDD who did the job well, and enthusiastically, folks who failed out of that crew were not moved to alternative training programs. Instead, they were moved *back* to the The Arc's internal cleaning crew.

Although this move saved money as paying the crew minimum wage to clean the agency's administrative building was less expensive than pay-ing an outside vendor a premium price, the building was shabby and dirty. Worse, it failed to advance the goals of the people we served. *Did the folks on the internal cleaning crew even want cleaning jobs?* From the results, I suspected they did not.

The board, prior to my hiring, had set as a goal expanding The Arc's employment training programs and options from cleaning and landscap-ing to, additionally, culinary arts and retail skills. The Arc NLC was not the only provider of IDD services trying to improve its track record for training people with IDD and helping them to find gainful employment. Many of my industry colleagues were launching training ventures aimed at accomplishing the same goal. However, many of the training enter-prises would launch ambitiously and then quickly shutter because too much money was flying out the door.

From a service perspective, employment services for people with IDD clearly were broken. If we were going to change minds, if we were going to move our community from low to high expectations, if we were going to establish standards for work performance for people with IDD that led to real career success, then true organizational transformation had to occur. It was here that the need for excellence starkly emerged, and while we had more questions than answers in those days, we realized that without a total transformation, we would fail.

It was a fairly easy idea to sell to the people we served and to the board and to the team: What if people with IDD, among the most underemployed and most marginalized people in the world, might themselves change the world with excellent performance? If we really believed in our mission and vision, in equality for people with IDD, then excellence was possible—and only excellence would do.

CEOs build careers on transformation. This certainly was not the first time I'd encountered things that needed fixing. Supply chains, delivery glitches, team building, quality shortfalls—none of these were new. Why couldn't the people we serve build careers on transformative excellence as well?

In those early days with The Arc, of course, employment services were not the only area of our organization that needed attention. As I familiarized myself with the agency and its team, I reviewed the stages of plan-building discussed earlier many, many times. Carefully, I continued to inventory The Arc NLC's strengths and challenges: What were The Arc NLC's patterns of failure? What were its patterns of success? What would be the resources required to face the challenges, to embrace the strengths, and to grow excellence?

The costs of some of our shortcomings have already been mentioned. Worker's compensation insurance premiums, for example, had topped $300,000 annually. Beyond that, over time, due to scheduling inefficiencies was costing another $100,000. A billing gap resulting from a lack of communication between operations and finance looked like $60,000 but, ultimately, had proved to be closer to $200,000. And doing the right thing, paying people with IDD minimum wage, was significantly contributing to our troubles. But taking inventory is important for a reason.

The Arc also had its strengths. Our finance and technology and in-home supports departments were performing well, led by highly skilled leaders who possessed the talents essential for building processes, services, and revenue growth. The board and my predecessor had put all these things into place. The agency's in-home supports director, for instance, was so personable she could bring in contracts at will. *If only the department itself was more profitable, I mused.*

My gut told me something was awry. As I evaluated our strengths and our weaknesses, it didn't make sense that one of our strongest directors would be posting such a weak bottom line. So, one afternoon, while sitting in my office stewing over the state's lackluster reimbursement rates, funding cuts, and flat-funding patterns, I picked up the phone and called the regional director of Connecticut's Department of Developmental Services. "At $26 per hour, we can barely cover our costs," I said. I tried to sound quizzical rather than accusatory. The director seemed surprised. "The rate is $28," she said. "You mean you aren't getting that?"

It probably was the quickest revenue problem I'd ever solved. Of course, the remaining challenges were not going to be addressed so easily. But I had managed to buy a little more time. Sometimes, intuitive, persistent CEOs get lucky ....

Our fundamental problems, it seemed, lay in quality assurance and operational details and dysfunctional teaming. Yet, despite our challenges, the community loved our big heart.

R. Bud Whipple had taught me well in an inverse kind of way. Rather than thinking about costs, I was looking for savings and revenue. *Remember Talibah? Taking her up on her offer, I did ask for help.* I asked the leadership team to establish a Safety Committee, and we charged it with reducing on-the-job injuries.

Even today, I know when the Safety Committee has met because maintenance software alerts flood my e-mail box. No fan of e-mail, I smile, nevertheless. The Safety Committee, hard at work, translates into more secure facilities, improved working conditions, and lower insurance premiums that hold potential for team incentives. And so, within one year of getting to work, the Safety Committee helped The Arc reduce its Worker's Compensation costs dramatically, freeing up a $200 incentive for every employee in the agency.

And what about quality and training and teamwork? Solving problems requires that we ask the right questions. If I was not going to be the person leading the effort to bridge The Arc's quality and training gap, then who would? Understanding we wanted only the best expertise, the kind of expertise that would help us achieve excellence in service delivery scores, I again approached the regional director.

"*Who is the best service delivery professional in the region?*"

The regional director suggested that I call Emma, who at that time was herself running a small agency called Seacorp, Inc. "If I were looking to improve service delivery," the director said, "I'd give Emma a call. I know she has helped many agencies to improve their service platforms."

To my surprise, Emma readily agreed to meet for coffee, and when I asked what her consulting fee would be to help The Arc train a crack staff and reconfigure its service models, Emma waved me off. "If it means people with IDD will live better lives," she said, "that's all that matters. Don't worry about paying me." In the ensuing months, Emma graciously mentored our staff. And she also mentored me. I remain grateful to her today.

It is often said that we get what we pay for, but I happen to disagree. When it comes to excellence, obsession with cost can cut both ways: Sometimes you do get what you pay for, and sometimes you pay too much. In Emma's case, pro bono consulting proved to be an unanticipated gift. Emma's work was so good that I offered her a job.

"I would love to," Emma said, "but I don't want to leave my team behind." Seacorp, Inc., where Emma had worked for more than a decade, employed a tightknit crew—a crew Emma had built and trained exceedingly well. Seacorp's quality scores were excellent. Certainly, they were measurably better than ours. I told Emma to call me if she ever changed her mind about working for The Arc. Although she called often, because we had become close friends, my offers of employment (often made in jest) were likewise jokingly rebuffed.

Until the day when they were not. Emma's board of directors was aging. Most had been there when Seacorp was founded at the time Connecticut began shutting down some of its institutions in the 1950s. All the board members had at one time had adult children living in an institution called Seaside in Waterford, Connecticut. As they established community homes for their offspring while Seaside was shuttered, the parents formed a nonprofit agency to recruit and train staff and maintain the homes they'd bought via fundraising: eight well-maintained properties along Connecticut's shoreline. They'd called it Seacorp, Inc.

But now, Connecticut's decades-long rocky relationship with its non-profit human service providers had taken a toll on Seacorp. While the agency was handily in the black and well-respected, its bottom line was shrinking. Seacorp still had a healthy cash reserve, but its directors were concerned about the agency's long-term prospects.

"My board is talking merger," Emma told me one day. They have charged me with talking with several providers about that and reporting back.

"Why don't you let me look at your books," I offered. "You've helped us, Emma. Who knows? Maybe I can find something that will help you?"

Emma agreed. Both Murray, The Arc's Chief Financial Officer, and I perused Emma's spreadsheets. Murray found a couple of areas where he thought Seacorp could make adjustments to weather the ongoing fiscal storm. I found a few as well. Murray had been friends with Emma for nearly 20 years, so we sat with her and relayed what we'd found. Murray and I believed Seacorp could survive. "The problem," I told Emma,

> is that your costs are rising and your income is flat. You've done a good job of holding the line, but without a cash infusion, without assuming additional service platforms, you're going to run out of money in about, oh, I'd say, three years. You need to invest in infrastructure and expand your programming beyond residential services.

Emma thanked us and went back to her board to discuss our findings. Their response surprised us all. The Seacorp Board of Directors asked what The Arc NLC thought about a merger. Seacorp's Board didn't want to expand services. They didn't want to risk adding infrastructure to do it. So, as the law and ethics require, I told the Seacorp Board that I'd need to take the proposal back to our own board.

Personally, I liked the idea. Seacorp's cash would buy us time as we sought to erase the red ink in our employment services—providing we invested in a real enterprise or two and didn't rashly spend the cash without making fundamental changes to our service structure. Extra cash also would give us something else we desperately needed: technology. And, best of all, Seacorp had talent. We needed Emma's expertise, and the expertise of her team.

As fallout from the Great Recession pounded Connecticut's nonprofits, shrinking tax revenues post-Recession came home to roost. While other nonprofits scrambled for cash, The Arc NLC (having absorbed Seacorp) found itself in a robust cash position.

The Arc NLC's Board of Directors wanted data, so Murray began running numbers, nimbly putting together his spreadsheets. It did not take long for all of us to realize that The Arc and Seacorp, Inc. really would be stronger together. By combining our finance departments, and by anticipating the placement of Seacorp folks into training positions at The Arc, the savings—combined with Seacorp's cash reserve—collectively totaled about $500,000 annually. Presented with our findings, both boards of directors voted for merger.

As fallout from the Great Recession continued to pound Connecticut, other nonprofits scrambled for cash. But The Arc NLC (having absorbed Seacorp) found itself in an enviable position compared to its peers. Postmerger, The Arc had invested much of the Seacorp cash reserve into technology, making our operations highly efficient. Combined with new technologies, Emma's efforts paid off significantly in the quality department: The Arc's quality service review scores with state regulators increased from around 88 to 97 percent, and then 99 percent, and finally reached perfect scores of 100 percent.

Because Emma had taken over The Arc's training curricula, supplementing the work of the Safety Committee and, postmerger, overseeing it, Worker's Compensation premiums continued to inch downward. With Murry and Emma working closely and communicating—and with the addition of Alice*, whose job was to track the accounts of services delivered against payments from our contractor, the State of Connecticut— The Arc realized $100,000 then $150,000 and then (as noted) $200,000 more in revenues due to its improved billing and quality processes.

The bottom line, while not exactly robust, stabilized the agency even as other nonprofit contractors increasingly struggled. And, as The

Arc's quality scores improved, more and more participants and families expressed interest in our services. Thanks to Emma's deftness with scheduling and her solid training talent, morale rallied, turnover fell, and overtime costs shrank—saving yet another $100,000 annually. Postmerger, as other providers continued to struggle, The Arc NLC, flush with Seacorp's cash and talent, grew by $3 million in billable revenues.

Ongoing state cuts and freezes continued to hand us budgetary wild cards every year. Despite The Arc NLC's turnaround from deficit to overage, annual surpluses proved slim, even by nonprofit standards, from about $100,000 to $300,000 net annually. Most of Connecticut's providers of services to people with IDD fared worse. A majority were in the red, some deeply, and a couple of them shut their doors.

At a time when some providers found themselves implementing pay cuts, The Arc was able to function leaner and more pragmatically. Morale continued to improve as, during the next three years, the agency continued to pay out modest incentives while other agencies found themselves laying off staff and reducing wages. It was during this period that The Arc's quality service scores hit 100 percent—a true measure of excellence.

Significant strategic challenges remained. The participant wage gap, for example, the difference between what the state of Connecticut paid The Arc to train people with IDD for community employment, and the wages that The Arc paid to people with IDD working in its vocational training programs, continued to grow as more participants joined the program. Though The Arc, as a nonprofit agency, was averaging $100,000 to $300,000 in annual surpluses, the wage gap for its employment training programs was inching over $100,000 per year.

Eventually, the gap would drive the agency into unsustainable deficit. Freezing program admissions might have been one strategy to stall losses, but the board had charged me with *growing* the employment program. Placing people into community employment was central to our mission. We needed to figure out how to do it well, with excellence—and we had to do it sooner, not later.

Fortunately, the Seacorp merger, along with the newfound operational efficiencies it brought, continued to buy us time. What we had to do now was pivot our employment services, essentially finding a way to put people to work in an industry that had failed to make any progress in two decades of trying.

Thanks to the strategic thinking of our board of directors, we had several important resources. The earmark grant had funded, additional to the kitchen, a small adjacent retail space; and there were the existent lawn crew and cleaning crews. In resolving to address a 20-year employment challenge, the board had decided doubling down in diversified vocational training options was the way to go.

The time had come for a plan: The Arc needed to launch a vocational training enterprise in the new kitchen that would produce results, that is, gainful employment placements for people with IDD among community employers. We needed to retool our lawn and cleaning options as well. Again, I took an inventory, but this time more specifically rather than globally: *What were our patterns of failure in employment?* While we were making good progress overcoming many of The Arc's operational challenges due to building ever more efficient operations and designing ever better trainings, we still were not placing people into community employment consistently.

What were our patterns of success? The community loved us. Participants loved us. Their families loved us.

On the other hand, we had burned some bridges by talking a good game without doing a great job at vocational training. *What were our resources for excellence?* We had that brand-new kitchen, debt free, thanks to the grant. We had technology and a growing IT team to help with e-commerce. And now, postmerger, we had a highly skilled leadership team. This is the kind of good fortune CEOs don't find every day. I felt a real duty to the board, which had envisioned the new kitchen, and to the team, who had heroically rallied to save costs and improve performance and worked gamely with great heart to turn things around.

We didn't yet have a chef, so we began our search for one. This was challenging on several fronts: Many people who applied for the position were talented, but they weren't natural coaches. I hired a few people who were enthused, but their depth and breadth in culinary arts proved thin. When we did find a real chef or two, the candidates lacked passion for working with people who have IDD.

It took longer than I'd imagined or would have preferred; but finally, a talented chef answered one of our many job postings, a man who with his wife had adopted several children with disabilities. And he really was an amazing chef. Chef Jack* set about cooking his heart out. He began doing it all as a means of helping us to find our culinary purpose: pastries, box lunches, pies, and filled breads.

As Chef Jack's work progressed, the community embraced our products. In the years prior to The Arc NLC's transition into The Arc ECT, the agency had built a reputation around Chef Jack's excellent chocolate chip cookies. We sold a lot of them. Unfortunately, they weren't exactly profitable because, as popular as the cookie was, given the price point we needed to hit, it didn't fly off the shelves. Too many consumers found the cookies too expensive.

I beat myself up about not having a clear vision forward. We needed a plan, but the small retail store located beside the bakery was not in a high traffic zone. So, the retail operation, which had been a big part of the board's original dream, wasn't a bona fide retail location in my opinion. It was a great training resource, but I was not going to invest the few and precious resource dollars we had to launch a store that I knew would fail.

Is timing everything? Sometimes. About six months prior, I'd been sitting in my back yard reading *The Day*, our regional newspaper out of New London, when I spied an article about a group of retired for-profit business executives who'd started, in their retirement, a nonprofit advisory group called the Mentoring Corps for Community Development (MCCD). I'd been so impressed that I'd saved the article. I'd actually taken it to work and set it in the middle of my desk. My instincts told me that these folks could help The Arc get its training enterprises off the ground, help us to turn fledgling programs into real businesses.

Sometimes, I felt remiss for not having called MCCD. I would stand over my desk and look down at the article. I'd stand there, gazing at the news clipping, chiding myself for not picking up the phone. And then, as in one of those dreams one has night after night that stops just short of resolution, I'd remind myself of the problem I had. *I don't know what question to ask!*

Finally, my board president, Rick, took me aside. "You need to take a vacation, kid," he said.

I have had many mentors in my life. So many people, from newspaper editors like the late MJ Schneider of *The Boyertown Area Times*, who taught me the ropes in my teens, to people like Franklin and Mark Bricklin, the brilliant editor-in-chief of *Prevention* magazine, have been generous teachers. Yet, of them all, Rick is the one who taught me the most. From handling personnel dilemmas to wielding power to getting tough or going easy, Rick counseled me like a treasured older brother or a father, even. I hadn't realized it, but Franklin's harsh lessons about working 24/7, along with a childhood steeped in a poverty of expectation, had set me up for the presumption that grinding it out was the only way to get the job done.

As in so many instances, Rick taught me there is a better way.

He wouldn't listen to my excuses. "We are losing money every day!" I told him. "How can I go on vacation *now*? I've got to get the employment program into the black!"

Rick chuckled. "The only thing you've convinced me of is that *you really do need a vacation*! Clear your calendar for no less than a week. Then go home and forget about us. I don't care if you do nothing but sit on your porch! Just go home and forget about this place."

So ingrained was my poverty of expectation that the idea of planning a vacation was beyond me. I had no clue how to take a vacation. So, I did, in fact, clear my calendar, go home, and spend a week sitting on my deck.

A funny thing happened on day three. It was about three o'clock in the afternoon, and I was sitting in the sunshine, reading a book. I was bored, so I walked into the house, grabbed a beer from the refrigerator, opened it and walked back outside. Just as I sat down, I heard a crash. From a ridge rising just beyond my backyard emerged a massive 10-point buck. The white-tailed deer looked down at me from about 12 yards away as if to say, what are *you* doing here?

I sat transfixed. "*What a vacation!*" I felt as if I were sitting in the middle of a greeting card. Then, its message delivered, the buck turned and ambled away. (How interesting is a woman who doesn't know how to take a vacation anyway?)

Why am I so stressed? I took a sip of beer. I certainly was stressed.

You're stressed because you have a kitchen, and you have a chef—but you don't know what product to make.

That was it. That absolutely was the source of my stress. *That was the problem I had!* The time had come to move the agency's training enterprises onto real profit tracks. We needed a business plan. But to create a business plan, I needed to know what product(s) Chef Jack and his kitchen crew should focus upon. What was our hook going to be?

The mentors! Finally, I knew what my question was! The first thing I was going to do the following Monday was call MCCD. In the meantime, I was going to take a vacation. I called the Groton Boat Club, signed up for a membership, and kayaked up the Mystic River every day for the next four days.

The following Monday, I picked up the phone.

When the day arrived for our meeting with MCCD, my team walked into a back room at The Arc where a jovial gray-haired man named Dick sat waiting at a small conference table. After the introductions, Dick got down to business.

"How can I help you?" he said.

Dick listened to the standard spiel about the founding of The Arc. I explained the dilemma of paying minimum wage. "Doing the right thing is not optional," I told Dick. "We have a talented team," I told him. "We can pretty much do anything. We have two international marketers and a bank marketer working here. Nobody works here because they have to. We work here because we want to, and while nobody is getting rich, The Arc pays better than a lot of nonprofits. To the extent that we are able, we invest in talent. Sometimes people come here hoping to hide, but it doesn't work. If you're not at the top of your game, this team will vote you off the island!"

Dick smiled. "Tell me about your business."

"We have a kitchen," I told him. "We have a chef. We need to establish a profit-track business. Here's our problem: We need to make an informed decision about which product to bring to market. Can you help? We have some resources, but not a whole lot. Trial and error won't work. We have to get it right the first time."

Dick smiled broadly. "Congratulations," he said, "You're the first nonprofit we've sat down with who knows what their problem is!"

Some weeks later, as planned, we reconvened with Dick and MCCD at The Arc's employment center. As Chef Jack made what he thought were his most marketable options, our friends from MCCD gladly sampled each treat, took copious notes and greatly enjoyed their volunteer assignment.

The next time he called, Dick informed us that he and Sydney, another retired MCCD executive, would be taking us on. Both men had spent three months assessing and surveying the snack industry on The Arc's behalf.

Following their research, Dick and Sydney had discovered The Arc's best shot at success did indeed lay in its chocolate chip cookie. But the snack purveyors did not think the large, chewy cookie that we were focused on at the time—delicious as it was—had sufficient profit margin nor an acceptable shelf life to hit industry profit markers. We need a smaller, crunchy cookie, 12 cookies to a pack, 10 packs to a case. Dick and Sydney had quizzed the region's snack distributors and relayed to us the industry markers we'd have to be able to hit to move the cookies along to a profit track.

Over the next six months, with the help of many, many community partners including MCCD, as well as supporters as diverse as our regional Chambers of Commerce, United Way of Southeastern Connecticut, the Community Foundation of Eastern Connecticut, Dominion Energy and ShopRite grocery stores, we moved steadily toward our goal. Only one problem remained to be solved, and it occupied my thoughts day and night: No matter how hard we tried, we couldn't get the cost of our cookies to break even or turn a profit. Labor costs were killing us.

In trying to make the enterprise work, we hit some amusing roadblocks, and some confounding ones too. At one point, a benevolent vendor offered us free, prepackaged cookie dough. *"A gift!" I thought.* By now, though, my team had gotten the Excellence Thing down. I didn't have to repeat it anymore. Sometimes, I heard them say it themselves, often to new employees who found working at The Arc a lot more like working for a for-profit than a nonprofit.

Don't get me wrong: The agency still had plenty of heart. Kinder, more invested people in those days (and today) cannot be found. But excellence by now had become a way of life. The team would get kind of insulted on behalf of our participants and families if newcomers sloughed off, telling them: "If you're not going to bring your A-Game, don't bother showing up."

As I sat at my desk imagining grand success with my free cookie dough, a knock sounded on the door jamb. Celeste* looked pensive. "Can I talk to you?" she said.

"Come on in!"

Celeste looked so troubled that I worried she might have gotten a job offer elsewhere and was coming to reluctantly give notice. She was my valued assistant.

"You know how you're always talking about excellence ..." she began.

"Yeah," I agreed. "What's going on?

"It's the cookie dough," she said.

"What about it?"

"It has preservatives," she said. "I don't think it's right for our customers, for our participants, for people with autism. A lot of parents don't want to feed their kids food with preservatives anymore. I wouldn't feed these cookies to my kids."

"Wow," I said. "But it solves all our problems. It gets us to profitability!"

"You can't do it," she said earnestly. "You're the one who's always telling us that everything we do has to be excellent! The cookie we *have* is excellent. And it's all natural! So, we *have to stick with excellence*! You have to find a way. *You're the one who taught us that*!"

Celeste smiled. She turned toward her own office, then paused for a parting shot: "We learned it from you!"

I got up from my desk. I made my way out of The Arc's parking lot in Norwich and then crossed an adjacent scratch of asphalt belonging to our neighbors, the dentists, who keep our smiles bright. Crossing Lafayette Street where an imposing black iron gate opens into Yantic Cemetery, I passed through, seeking to commiserate with the souls lying there, as I often do when needing to clear my head.

As I ambled down path after dusty path lined with flags and tombs and crypts, with urns and tablets and obelisks, and here and there a textured, concrete tree stump elegantly commemorating a life well lived, my befuddlement transformed to a mantra. Celeste was right. We had the product we needed. The problem I wanted was the challenge of selling a cheaper cookie, one whose dough was free. The problem I had was more complex. How would we make the excellent cookie affordable? *"What on earth do I do now?"* I asked myself. *"What do* we *do now?"*

The Secrets of Chapter 7

- MENTORS ARE MANDATORY! Don't wait. Create a list of folks you believe you can learn from, and then prioritize finding a mentor or two for your ongoing executive development.
- EMBRACE REALITY. Solve the problem you have, not the problem you want.
- LEAD WITH MISSION. If you don't drive forward with your inherent values, your mission, that is, *people with IDD are equal and therefore deserve equal treatment in housing, technology, and employment—including minimum wage—*you will fall short of excellence. If you don't commit to excellence with honesty and humility, you will also will miss all the benefits excellence confers upon your executive development, your career trajectory ... and your life.
- FOCUS. Define what must happen. Just as important, obtain the resources, whatever they are, to make it happen. **Develop a courageous perspective for embracing the solutions of a given problem and the resources for addressing it, no matter how daunting.**

For Discussion

- CRUNCH TIME. What's the one thing you keep avoiding? What's your own personal cookie dough dilemma? How is it holding back your organization's progress?
- MAKE IT HAPPEN. How can your organization's values inform your dreams? How can your organization's values inform your participants' and/or customers' dreams? Your team's? The best outcomes? Who and what do you need to make these dreams—and excellent outcomes—a reality?

CHAPTER 8

The New Nonprofit Model—Microbusiness and Mission

Can you say no to a donor?

The nature of charitable gifting, with its requisites generosity and gratitude, can make demurring seem counterintuitive. Yet, as difficult as it can be to tap into philanthropic largesse, it is just as important to know when doing so might prove problematic.

According to Veritus Group, some reasons a charity might say no to a gift include:

1. **MISSION DRIFT.** "You say no when a donor wants to give a gift that would completely alter your mission."
2. **OVERREACH.** "You say no when a donor wants to microdirect their gift and be involved in the implementation of that gift."
3. **MANIPULATION.** "You say no when a donor wants to give a gift and have it further the interests of a business partner."
4. **OVEREXTENSION.** "You say no to a funder, whether it be an individual, foundation, corporation or government that for a small grant makes you jump through so many hoops the time spent on obtaining the grant outweighs the value of the grant." (Perry 2016)

Most nonprofits have their own acceptance policies based on mission and vision statements, and generally they resemble the above-mentioned with minor variations. For example, The Arc ECT would reject gifts, offers, or funds from organizations whose objectives and background undermine the agency's mission, vision, and values of equality and full partnership for people with IDD.

While many gifts, particularly those from private individuals, offer cash or items based on what is needed, still others have a specific goal in mind such as honoring an individual in a meaningful way or supporting specific aspects of social change. A founding family with many surviving siblings once donated to The Arc ECT a portrait of their brother, painted by an artist of note in the region. No one in the family had space for a painting that size. Further, if one family member were to keep the painting, which one would it be? So now a wonderful painting hangs in a gathering space at The Arc with a plaque honoring the young man and his ability to light up a room and readily befriend the folks he met. Creative solutions can benefit all concerned.

The Arc ECT has not had many gifting dilemmas in its 70-year history, but when we did, it involved nothing less than chocolate chip cookie dough, the cookie dough that Celeste told me we could not, under any circumstances, accept. That was the day she stood in the doorway so tentatively, and I still appreciate her honesty and her candor despite her discomfort.

After Celeste had left my office that day, I'd walked through a nearby cemetery pondering it all. What to do with the largesse? Other concerns ran through my mind, too: If making cookies provided vocational and occupational experience for people with IDD, counting cups and teaspoons and tablespoons and eggs and using industrial mixers and depositors and filling empty cookie bags—all activities that prepared people for a host of community jobs—then premade cookie dough kind of defeated the purpose of our vocational goals.

Still, I had to consider all angles. *What if hand-making the cookies as we were doing would prove to be the single most critical factor precluding our selling them at a competitive price? What if premade dough was the only way to bridge the pricing gap? What if, in saying no thanks to the dough, we offended our generous donor who had offered far more than cookie dough to The Arc ECT through the years?*

I'd concluded my walk past a beautiful bronze sculpture, a grave marker. Kneeling, the contemplative figure of a woman prays as the veil gracefully covering her head flows to her feet. With elevated spirits thanks to the fresh air and bucolic surroundings, yet well-aware I'd solved no problems, I'd walked back to my office. (I realize not everyone might find a walk through a graveyard buoying, but a sense of peace and purpose with those souls gone before always leaves me feeling calmer and more focused.)

Like many insights, the real breakthrough, when it came, happened around 3 a.m. As I lay awake figuring out what to do, it dawned on me that there was some irony in losing sleep over cookie dough.

Moreover, I was embarrassed to realize how elementary the solution was when, finally, it came. "You know how to do this!" I thought suddenly. "The solution—simple marketing—is something you've done for years!"

The answer now was clear: We would do a blind market test. In my publishing days, we did market tests all the time. They were not difficult. We would do a simple test, and the results would tell us how excellent our cookie really was (or not).

If our cookie stood up to an impartial test of excellence, then I had no choice but to go to our donor and decline the dough. Still troubling was a concern that The Arc's cookie, due to its handcrafting by people who at times possess motor skills requiring extra time to mix, form, and bake, could ultimately prove too expensive. But that was a different problem altogether.

Right now, the question at hand was simple and its solution lay rooted in the excellence I'd so often preached, as Celeste had so tactfully pointed out. Was our cookie the best cookie ... or was it not? R. Bud Whipple crossed my mind, but I brushed those thoughts away. I would not let worries about price get in the way of excellence. First, I had to establish whether The Arc's cookie *was really excellent.*

Celeste knew as soon as she saw me the next morning that my mood had shifted. "I've got it!" I told her. Like several of us, Celeste had worked in marketing prior to joining our team.

"We're going to do a blind taste test with the cookies!" I said. "If people pick our cookie, if you're right that ours really is better, then I'll figure out a way to deliver the news to our donor. And then we'll all figure out how to make our cookie work, pricewise."

Celeste smiled broadly. "I'm not worried," she said. "You'll see." And so, we organized the blind taste test. Chef Jack made several batches of each cookie. Celeste, well-schooled in market testing, carefully put together a check-the-box survey allowing our taste-testers to evaluate appearance, taste, crunch, and overall preference. Meticulously, she separated the cookies into single-serve bags with coded labels.

We had no trouble finding volunteers. Team members in two locations volunteered to sample the free cookies with Celeste standing by. When the board of directors discovered what we were up to, we were ribbed good-naturedly. The board wanted in on the tasting action. Without hesitation, Celeste threw together a third test. Board members ate their cookies at the next meeting and filled out the survey.

Murray took the results and put a spread sheet together so the data would be easy to read. I opened Murray's e-mail when it landed in my inbox with expectation and hope.

Celeste was appropriately triumphant when I walked into her office, a big smile on my face. "You're right, I told her. Our cookie's better." Out of a couple of dozen surveys, only one person had chosen the donor's cookie.

Now, to face the next challenge: How best to break the news to our donor?

I decided to give Dick a call. "I need your advice," I told him. As I relayed the story to Dick, I could sense he was amused. "If I can have 20 minutes of your time," I said, "just name the day and the hour. I'm willing to come over to your house to make things more convenient."

Dick promptly offered a time and date for later that week.

On Thursday, I pulled into the drive of a seaside home on the Connecticut shoreline. Having greeted Dick, his wife, and their small dog, I got to work. "I need you to take the taste test," I explained to Dick, "and then I need a little advice."

Dick did not complain at the prospect of being required to eat a couple of chocolate chip cookies. He picked up one and dutifully filled out the survey; then, he ate the other one and did the same on the second sheet of paper. "It's not even close," he said. "This cookie is superior."

I looked at the code. It was The Arc's Classic Crunch Chocolate Chip Cookie.

"Here's what I want to do," I told Dick. "I want to put the results of all the taste tests into one spreadsheet. And then I want to send that to Ralph*, our longtime donor and a prominent community leader. I will explain to Ralph that we have a dilemma. His dough is not an all-natural product. For our audience, that can be a problem. Ours is all natural!"

Dick spoke encouragingly. "That's a good plan," he said. "If I were Ralph, I wouldn't be offended in the least. It's a respectful approach. Who knows? Ralph might have an idea we haven't thought of!"

As it happens, Dick was right. Within a very short time of calling Ralph, leaving a message on his cell phone and following up with our market-test data via e-mail, my phone rang. It was Ralph. I was relieved to hear in his voice that Ralph also seemed amused. He sounded a lot like Dick, actually. The two lifelong businessmen clearly enjoyed sharing their time and their knowledge and helping us figure our way through a challenge.

"How much does your cookie cost?" Ralph asked. "Too much," I said with mirthful irony. "They're about fifty cents apiece. How about yours?"

"Twenty-two cents," Ralph replied. "I'll tell you what: You get your cookie down to twenty-two cents apiece, and I will sell YOUR cookies on my snack truck." My voice broke a little as I thanked Ralph profusely.

This was the break we had been seeking. Ralph owned a chain of food trucks* on the Eastern seaboard. Many people approached Ralph on a daily basis asking him to sell their products. Ralph's truck space was so coveted that one aspiring entrepreneur, on learning that I had Ralph's cell number, said, in an awed voice: "My God, you've got the number to the Bat Phone!"

And so, I did, and now we were making good progress in our cookie caper. "We'll do it," I told Ralph. "Let me get my team together and do a little brainstorming."

The first thing I did upon hanging up from my conversation with Ralph was call Dick. "I'll be over tomorrow," Dick said. "Let's figure this thing out."

"We need to take advantage of someone else's marketing dollars," I said to Dick. "We're doing something wrong, but we don't know what it is."

"I agree!" Dick said.

"Maybe our research to date has taken us as far as it can. Maybe we need a new model—not a regional model but a national one."

"That could be the case!" Dick agreed.

I mused further: "Who's the industry leader, nationally, not locally?" I asked Dick.

We have a gourmet cookie. If we can get the price point right, people will surely buy our cookie over a national brand. Local is better, and our cookies mean jobs for people with IDD at minimum wage or better! We have a compelling message. What do you think of Big Meadow Brands*, Dick?

"I think that's a good one to try to match," Dick said. "I'll tell you what. On my way over there tomorrow, I will pick up a pack of Big Meadow chocolate chip cookies."

"Perfect," I said. "Let me get the team together."

I sat at my desk for a little while. I went over the names of our agency's leaders in my head. I wanted the most creative people on the team at the table tomorrow, no matter their backgrounds or duties. I already knew that collectively my team was smarter than I was; now, I wanted to get the smartest solutions onto the table for discussion.

The following afternoon, we sat around the board table in my office. My hand-picked team had been told only that we needed to do some brainstorming. I doubt anybody was surprised when Dick walked in. With a flourish, he set a Big Meadow cookie package in the middle of the table.

"You're here today," I said to my team,

because you're the most creative people we've got. Ralph has given us an amazing gift. If we can get the price of our cookie to twenty-two cents, Ralph will carry our cookies in all his snack trucks. Frankly, it's the big break we've been waiting for.

Murray tells me our cookie costs fifty cents. Over time, as we sell more, the price should come down because with this product price and volume are inversely related. But to sell a lot, we have to get onto those trucks. To do that, our cookies must cost less than half of what they cost today.

"I'll bet Big Meadow Brands spends a couple of million dollars a year marketing their chocolate chip cookie," I speculated. "Well, folks, we don't have a million dollars. So, let's learn on Big Meadow's dime. What is it about the Big Meadow cookie's packaging and marketing that we're missing?"

"*We're gathered here together today to say goodbye to an unprofitable cookie…*" I intoned. And everyone laughed.

I didn't want people to feel stressed at the magnitude of what we needed to do. Unless we could free-associate in a safe space, we weren't going to succeed. **A coach once counseled me: "You're very intense. People can get intimidated by that. Fortunately, you've got a great sense of humor. Use it. Use it to counteract the intensity."**

Such valuable advice! In guiding your team to a safe space for creating things, don't underestimate humor. It works.

As a team, we sat at the table in my office looking at Big Meadow's packaging. We checked the weight. People simply threw out ideas, randomly, suggesting things that Big Meadow might know that we did not. We checked the size of the bag. We reviewed the ingredients. Big Meadow's cookie also was all-natural, so we decided we'd probably chosen the correct product for comparison.

When I talk to audiences and tell the story of The Arc ECT Classic Crunch Chocolate Chip Cookie and how it came to be, I call to mind *2001, a space odyssey: "Remember the opening scene? The obelisk with the apes gathering round … everyone staring intently trying to figure out what the obelisk was about?"* That was my team and Dick and me with that package of Big Meadow cookies.

Like an obelisk with a secret, the package of Big Meadow cookies sat in the middle of the table while we circled it, staring at it. Murray spoke first. "I eat Big Meadow cookies all the time," he said. "Now I am realizing that ours are quite a bit bigger than theirs."

Aha! We needed to copy Big Meadow's cookie dimensions. That surely would save on price.

"How many cookies are in a Big Meadow package?" I asked. "And … by the way … let's measure them right now! I am pretty sure Murray is onto something here…."

Dick looked uncomfortable. He shifted in his seat. "I don't know how many cookies are in a bag," he said. "And we can't measure them right now."

"Why?"

Dick looked a bit hangdog. "I ate them all on the drive over here!"

When we stopped laughing, Seth*, our IT Chief, who had also worked in marketing and sales for many years before moving to nonprofit service, reached an arm across the table, grabbed the bag, examined it, and pointed to a number. "Fifteen per bag!" he exclaimed. Looking at Dick, he cracked: "No thanks to you!"

Dick had unwittingly proved to be a market test in his own right. It turns out that America has a love affair with cookies that sets us apart in the world. The average adult American eats 19,000 cookies in a lifetime, and that excludes cookies the individual might have eaten as a child (Daily Mail 2015). Americans eat 7 billion cookies a year, or about 1,000 cookies per person (The Cravory 2016).

Ralph had once expounded on our choice of product saying: "I'm awfully glad you guys chose to make cookies because people just love cookies! I don't know why, but I can't keep 'em on my trucks. They just fly outta there!" Among all those flying cookies is the supreme favorite, or America's favorite cookie. Once again, Dick and Sydney and our mentors had steered us well: Hands down, it's the chocolate chip. (Daily Mail 2015) Dick's love for cookies, particularly chocolate chip cookies, made him demographically American through-and-through.

Chef Jack spoke. "Let me go back to the kitchen," he said. Looking at Dick, he laughed. "I'll buy another bag of Big Meadow Cookies so I can measure them since these seem to have vanished! Let me see what we can do over in the kitchen."

"Let's start with the same dimensions and fifteen cookies to a bag," I told Jack.

Looking at Murray, I said, "Get what you need from Jack, then calculate the cost and let me know as soon as you can."

Murray nodded. "I can do that," he said.

I thanked everyone for their time.

We adjourned for about a week. Chef Jack sent his product information over to Murray, who called me as soon as his calculations were complete.

"Jack has it down to twenty-five cents," Murray said. "I know our calculations are correct. I'm sorry. We really can't get it lower than that. We've really tried."

"That's pretty close!" I told Murray. "In fact, I never thought we'd get that close on our first couple of tries. Let me call Ralph."

Ralph promptly returned the message left on the Bat Phone.

"Ralph," I said, "We've tried and tried, but we just can't get the price under twenty-five cents!"

Ralph didn't hesitate. "That's close enough!" he said. "But you need a good bag, and you need an FDA food label and a bar code before I can sell them."

"We have the bar code," I told Ralph. "Let me see what I can do about the other two things."

When I told Dick the good news, he said, "Let's do this right. You guys are nonprofit stars. Let me talk to our team at MCCD. Maybe we can track down a bag designer for you guys."

And so they did. The MCCD mentors called friends, made inquiries, and located both a professional who was certified to create Food & Drug Administration-approved food labels as well as an artist who had designed multiple bags for cookies sold all over the United States. The artist suggested we use paper coffee bags because that would reduce production costs by a lot—until our sales volume allowed us to go with a bigger printer who would customize the bags.

We took our mentors' advice. The only snag occurred when we realized Chef Jack was putting so much butter in the cookies it was bleeding through the bag. I didn't like the idea of changing a thing, but all those years in publishing were paying off as we reviewed our printing and bag options. We had the printer darken the background color of the bag just a little bit, and it worked. The butter could stay in the cookie, and the cookie would no longer visibly stain the darker-colored bag.

Ralph was delighted with our progress. He had just one more hoop for us to jump through. It was reasonable, and—if anything—would give our team more confidence and put our cookie in an even stronger market position. Ralph directed us to a firm that his company used for focus groups. It would cost $10,000, but if our cookie passed a national focus group taste test, just as it had done internally at The Arc, then Ralph really was going to sell our cookie. An added benefit would be an opportunity to test, at the same time, several bag designs that Dick's artist had put together. It was an offer we wisely accepted. (A local bank later gave us grant for $10,000 to cover the cost of the focus group.)

We really were gaining momentum.

Almost everyone, but not *everyone*, was pleased.

The Arc Eastern Connecticut's Classic Crunch Chocolate Chip Cookie won a blind taste-test in New London, CT, conducted by a national market research company. The same day, focus group participants chose this package design. The rigorous standards embraced by The Arc ECT ensured product excellence would prevail.

Murray didn't think a nonprofit could or should aspire to perform like a for-profit. Emma felt keeping people safe and walking with them as they lived their best life was a big enough job. She didn't want the distraction of microbusinesses. She saw the effort as mission drift. The board of directors, on the other hand, was excited and believed alternate revenues would help stabilize what had become alarming and increasingly erratic funding patterns for the agency.

Because safe space and teamwork and creative collaboration are so critical to success—whether an organization is a for-profit or a non-profit—one of my biggest challenges arises when key members of my team disagree with a strategic direction of The Arc ECT. How does a team-oriented executive navigate such a dilemma?

I looked at it this way: Emma and Murray and their teams had 20 years to place people with IDD into competitive employment. The IDD field itself had two decades to do better. We had failed. Even The Arc ECT's track record in employment services stood in contrast to our track record in every other service: Emma, for instance, had taken us from quality scores in the 80 percentile all the way to 100 percent in a few short years. That told me we were great at meeting the state's bureaucratic benchmarks. We were great, even, at being among the leaders in the field of IDD services in Connecticut—which was no small feat.

But neither government nor its bureaucracy are particularly adept at entrepreneurship. About half of our team, the true veterans, Emma and Murray included, were not accustomed to thinking entrepreneurially and resisted the idea of running a business alongside a human service agency. I reminded everyone that the strategic plan called for us to diversify revenues while fixing the broken employment model, and we'd all created that plan. Did anyone have a better idea? There was grumbling, but everybody agreed to move the project forward.

The public domain, in its judgment of our microbusiness launch, also proffered some mixed reactions. Every one of our funders loved the idea of a nonprofit behaving more like a for-profit. Local businesses cheered us on, bought and sold our cookies, and looked for ways to sponsor our events with ever-greater commitment. Long-time champions of rights for people with IDD, however, people who had been in the field all their lives and were considered experts and who were revered, even, were not universally pleased.

Remember Willowbrook? One aspect of this type of institutional abuse had been putting people with IDD to work at those institutions for little or no pay: feeding other people with IDD, cleaning floors and bathrooms, working in food service, doing direct service tasks. Remember sheltered workshops, where people performed rote tasks but never got promoted out of the job? Understandably, at least one national expert challenged us: "How is what you are doing different? If a person with IDD works for your organization, that is institutional employment."

In fact, we were different in three significant respects:

1. **WAGES.** The Arc ECT pays minimum wage, not subminimum wage or no wage at all.

2. **TRAINING VERSUS EMPLOYMENT.** If The Arc planned to employ a person with IDD *without creating a plan with that person* to find community employment, then it would indeed be guilty of institutional employment, albeit better paid. If, however, The Arc uses microbusinesses to ensure that people with IDD receive real-time, competitive vocational training in a real business setting, via a real economic platform and pressures (a bona fide business plan), then we will have done a far *better* job of training people for competitive employment than other providers. Indeed, if we moved the needle even a little on national placement averages, then we would be leading the field.

   Our goal was to deliver excellence in employment services in landmark fashion. Our goal was to prove that people with IDD are indeed capable of excellent performance. Our goal was to prove that people with IDD are capable of excelling in real jobs. **People can be forgiven for thinking our goal was to make great cookies, or to make money, but they would be mistaken. Our goal was to change universal opinion. Our goal was to change the world.**

3. **DIGNITY IN EXCELLENCE.** People with IDD are among the most marginalized in the world. But if I have IDD, and I make the best cookie you have ever eaten, then your view of my ability is forever changed. Excellence, for all its virtue, appeals especially in this case because of the extreme marginalization of people with IDD. At

the point that a customer realizes a person with IDD is making an excellent product, then the message conveyed becomes truly transformative. Excellence can change minds by flipping perceptions in ways that crush stereotypes. This is another way that The Arc ECT strives for excellence.

Our goal, always, is to achieve excellence. We aimed to stop repeating failure also. If we generated alternative and stabilizing revenue streams as our board had directed me to do, well then, all the better. Certainly, my bosses had every right to give me my marching orders. I answered to the board. Further, I did not believe that solving a problem that had plagued our field for two decades—training people with IDD for gainful employment—could be accomplished "the way we've always done it." If we gave people the tools they needed to do real jobs for real pay, *we would indeed have changed the world.*

If we failed to move people into community employment, our venerated leaders in the field were right: Then, we were nothing more than a glorified minimum-wage-paying sheltered workshop.

My hunch, though, was that a primary reason for our failure in training and placing people with IDD into competitive employment was *time.* We've discussed various reasons why employment success has proved so elusive for people with IDD, for their families and for providers. Along with all of those, it seemed to me that the vast array of abilities and differences among the people we served meant that all of us simply needed more time to train people who often presented with quite complex conditions.

Government's one-size-fits-all bureaucratic model (*Think: Marshall Plan*) does work in many respects despite our love for kicking that concept under the bus; however, for people with more complicated levels of vocational need, it does not. What I love about the microbusiness model we've created is that people with IDD can work in the businesses for as long as they need. A profit-track microbusiness can continue paying a person minimum wage, and it will not blow up the bottom line. There needs to be an understanding that, at some point, graduation has to happen. But people who need more time to succeed have it.

Consider the story of Sam*. We've served Sam for many years. Sam is quite capable, lives in his own apartment and has by now worked and excelled within every one of The Arc's microventures. For some years, every time Sam's case worker asked Sam if he wanted to move into community employment, Sam said yes. The caseworker would then request that The Arc find Sam community employment, which wasn't difficult. Sam's good nature, buoyant personality, self-presentation, and conversation skills are excellent.

Most people wouldn't guess Sam has IDD when first meeting him. About five times, The Arc placed Sam into competitive employment at his and his caseworker's request. Each time, in spite of everyone's enthusiasm and Sam's ability to do the job, Sam grew ever more anxious. Sam would then begin to decompensate. Sam's anxiety disorders would get the best of him, and soon he was having trouble getting out of bed, reporting for work, and would call his case manager and beg to return to The Arc.

The case worker would recommend that The Arc rehire Sam, which we would do. Sam was a terrific worker. He helped microbusinesses meet goals, and we always found him to be an asset on the team. But the reality was, Sam's trajectory was not average. After several years of doing every job in every microbusiness, Sam really had little left to learn.

And then Mohegan Sun Casino in Uncasville, CT, called to say they were looking for skilled line-prep chefs. Fully aware of The Arc's microventures, the Casino inquired whether we had any vocational candidates they might hire.

Again, we all sat down with Sam. We told him he was the best person for the job in our opinion. Did he want to give community employment another try? This would be his choice, not ours. Sam said he wanted to think about it, and we encouraged him to take his time contemplating.

Sam came back of his own accord a week or so later. He said he thought working as a line-prep chef was something that he was ready to do. Job coaches and counselors walked him through the training as they had done with Sam so many other times before. Sam went to work at Mohegan Sun. He was given a chef's coat and his own set of knives. Sam chopped thousands of lemons. He made hundreds of sandwiches.

Five years later, Sam has been nominated for "Most Helpful Employee" twice. He won the honor the last time he was nominated. He is popular in the kitchen at Mohegan Sun, where he continues to be employed, and his confidence and self-respect are things to behold.

For Sam, somewhere around the sixth time proved the charm. We will never know why this time the outcome proved different than before. Certainly, his co-workers and Mohegan Sun deserve credit for welcoming him and helping him to feel safe while learning and toiling there. Finding the right job and the right co-workers can challenge any one of us.

I would suggest also that, for people with IDD, employment training needs to be a forgiving process. People with IDD can indeed be fully employed. For some, a much longer training curve is required, and that training curve is not always connected to IQ or ability. People with learning delays might struggle with certain tasks and take exponentially longer to learn some things while grasping other concepts quicker than you or I might. The variables are as diverse as the people themselves, as diverse as you and me. Yet, once a task is mastered, a person with IDD might well perform more consistently or even outperform you or me.

As a person who entered IDD services without any understanding of the field, I have marveled at the infinite combinations of ability that I encounter daily among the people whom we serve. We've talked about the limitations of bureaucracy, and it is my belief that the time required for a person with significant challenges to be mainstreamed into a real community job—in many cases—is longer than the government is willing or able to fund. Enter the microbusiness, an excellent bridge between the nonprofit and for-profit sectors; also, an excellent bridge to success in training people with IDD for real jobs for real pay. ***With the proper supports, every person who wants a job can be fully employed.***

Thus, the team's concerns and the board's goals notwithstanding, The Arc ECT's microbusinesses were (and are) focused upon one thing and one thing only: How to affordably and practically train a person with IDD for a community job of his or her choosing—*however long that might take*. The job I might have wanted was the one that saw people prepared for real work when the funding ran out. That wasn't the job I had, though. Even today, many nonprofit IDD providers continue to do employment supports as they've always done. More and more, nonprofits claim to run microbusinesses. All too often, they are doing so without a proper business plan or a commitment to basic economics; hence, two decades of flat performance in placing people with IDD into real jobs remains a legacy.

What The Arc ECT's microbusinesses do is buy time for training via microbusiness break-even, or even profitable, performance. Because The Arc sets forth a goal that every microbusiness will be run on a profit track, a true economic platform based on real-world business dynamics is in play for each vocational participant. Because the bureaucratic, traditional jobs model simply doesn't work for too many people presenting with the complexity of IDD, The Arc ECT built a different one.

Alas, just as we began to hit our stride with the microbusinesses and were moving them ever so slowly toward viability, COVID-19 hit. If, as Dutch Leonard told us during Harvard's Nonprofit Crisis Management Workshop, the real measure of a nonprofit during crisis is whether it can thrive, then the microbusinesses needed to emerge from the pandemic stronger than before.

As the pandemic raged, I went back to my notes, where I had recorded a comment from Leonard: "*What do we do when no one knows what to do? The answers to the questions are a process…. What are the elements of process? Structure….*"

Understandably, the idea of making cookies and running businesses in a pandemic made Emma, whose primary responsibility is safety, quite nervous. She'd begun to come around on the microbusinesses themselves because they were proving effective in aiding job placements.

But I was convinced that the time for boldness, for thriving, had arrived. Keeping people safe didn't necessarily mean playing it safe business-wise. The time to invest was now. Counterintuitive though it might have seemed, at the height of the COVID pandemic, The Arc ECT made a strategic decision to invest in promoting a director of community enterprise to oversee the day-to-day operations of the microbusinesses. That would take some of the load off Emma, allowing her to focus solely on agency health and safety and PPE, a huge responsibility even absent a pandemic.

I had someone in mind for the community enterprise job, too. Following the merger of The Arc NLC and The Arc Quinebaug Valley, The Arc ECT found itself with not only its original cookie and lawn and cleaning ventures but with Quinebaug's small thrift shop and a recycling center. Eileen* had worked for The Arc Quinebaug for years and had been transferred to employment services postmerger. She'd also run her own business some years earlier.

The Arc Eastern Connecticut's recycling bins promote a clean and green image to encourage donations.

Within months, Eileen had the cookie business reorganized and a cookie factory buildout underway. Quinebaug's own training enterprises, The Emporium thrift shop and Donation Station, a recycling center which she rebranded, were in the black for the first time. Despite COVID-19, The Arc's microbusinesses had pivoted from passivity to aggressive pursuit of market share. As the pandemic began winding down, we realized a long-term dream with the completion of The Cookie Factory adjacent to The Emporium and Donation Station in a building acquired through the merger.

Among The Arc ECT's successful microbusiness pandemic pivots: The Redemption Center became a Donation Station. People still receive deposits for their bottles and cans; however, we also established dozens of drop sites throughout Eastern Connecticut where people can fill bins with their unwanted bottles and cans allowing the agency to convert these items into revenues for wages. The Emporium began pushing its wares through social media and no longer accepting whatever came in the door. As the shop got more selective, prices were raised modestly, and the shop began posting slim profits regularly. With Emma's help, participant employment schedules were managed more tightly, greatly boosting the bottom lines of all the businesses.

Perhaps you wondered, when Celeste challenged the strategic value of the generic cookie dough, why I didn't just eat the cookies and make an executive decision on which cookie really was best? Well, that might have been the problem I wanted. But it wasn't the problem I had.

I have a severe dairy allergy. All the butter Chef Jack was putting in those cookies would have made me terribly sick. I couldn't have eaten those cookies if I had wanted to. My own challenge with dairy products turned out to be serendipitous, an opportunity that opened the door to a best-practice solution, market tests, which allowed us to move forward boldly and confidently. Every minus can be turned into a plus.

The Secrets of Chapter 8

- EMBRACE OPPORTUNITY. When times get tough, seek not to survive but to thrive.
- BORROW IDEAS. If you know you're short of the mark and you don't know why; if you don't have a lot of cash for research; if you don't know the answer but you know the answer must be out there: Use alternate resources and creative pathways. Find answers and ideas by studying your competition and organizations and individuals who have deeper

pockets than you and have made the requisite cash investment to achieve marketing insights. Look at leaders in other
fields who have solved unique problems and brainstormed
innovative solutions: How did they do it? What part of their
approach can inform your own innovations?

- EXTEND INVITATIONS. Invite mentors. It can indeed be
lonely at the top. Don't make it worse. When you feel alone
in problem-solving, call the smartest people you know both
within your team and in your greater community. Bring the
best minds you can find to the table, create a comfortable
environment … and listen. *(Think: Brain Trust—and think it
often!)*
- CHALLENGE INDUSTRY ASSUMPTIONS. Have the
courage to embrace the facts. Don't be afraid to ask: What if
the thing everybody *thinks* is true … is not?

For Discussion

- WHERE ARE THE ANSWERS? Where are some unusual
and creative places you might look for answers to some of
your more vexing challenges? What is the one thing you are
most sure of? Why? Are you *sure*? How do you know?
- USE THE BRAINPOWER OF YOUR TEAM. Who are
your most creative players? Which members of your team
think differently and/or problem-solve with different styles
than you do? Remind yourself that you need these people *as
much as* those who might think like you and be more likely to
agree with you. How can you better harness the creativity of
your *whole* team? Are there people in your greater community
whose mindpower and creativity you can also tap?

CHAPTER 9

Tech Is Your Nonprofit Superpower

While The Arc's initial foray into technology was at first met with the teamwide trepidation most organizations face at the prospect of embracing tech, our journey was well-served by a sobering lesson borne of my publishing days. Quite a few years back, *Faith Journal's* "management" (i.e., suited fellows making decisions none of us were consulted about) had invested in critical customer data-collection software*.

The training process was long, and the learning curve longer still. As the software adoption progressed, longtime employees began to loudly and adamantly oppose the new technology. Walking around the building offered quick insight to the new software.

"It's not working … again!"

"Looks like the software is down … again."

"Not again!"

"I've been on the line with customer service for a half-hour now, and I'm still on hold!"

Franklin, now back at corporate, merely laughed in his charming way when I brought up the matter in a phone call one day. "People don't like change!" he said. Just prior to Franklin's buying the software, we had acquired a small mom-and-pop operation in a nearby Midwest town*. The entire workforce within the acquisition, newly relocated to our facility, complained incessantly about the good old days. Nobody at the small division with the so-called problem software was a fan of computers or technology. They had not really used tech before.

But then a colleague of Franklin's who had been transferred in to take over the division when Franklin was recalled to headquarters took me to lunch. I would be getting a big promotion, he told me. "And, by the way," he said, "that little division of complainers? They are going to be joining your team!"

I drove home that night with mixed feelings. The opportunity was apparent, but the new division was not a happy one. Introducing change was going to be challenging as the underperforming group did not want to hear that a new way of doing things lay ahead. They believed their products were just fine, and they were disinclined to change their processes. While the division was profitable, its products were dated, even quaint, and profit margins were shrinking every year. On the other hand, solving the riddle everyone was talking about now would now fall to me. *Did the software work or didn't it?*

Was it possible that Franklin and his team really had inadvertently bought a lemon in the data-collection system they had purchased? I had a hard time believing that. More likely, the team really did not like change. They pretty much complained about everything.

And yet....

The ongoing conversation in customer service was hard to ignore, and it was consistent. A few things troubled me about what I was seeing and hearing: The wait times on hold for tech support from the system's vendor were gumming up our ability to function optimally. The system crashed a lot, too. That didn't seem right to me. And it really affected productivity.

How best to sort it all out? And then it hit me: *Frieda**! **It was my job to ask the right questions, after all!**

Among the best customer service representatives with whom I've ever worked, then or now, was Frieda. Frieda knew her products, her customers, and her systems. Frieda often shared her opinions without any shellac, but you knew where you stood with Frieda.

Frieda was no-nonsense. Frieda liked her job, and she made it her business to know what she was talking about. Tomorrow, I'd sit with Frieda. I'd ask her to show me the software. How was it used? What was she trying to do with it, and was the software helpful in any way at all? In what ways, and when, was it less useful? Maybe I could tease out some information, glean a bit of insight.

I learned a lot the next day, just as I had hoped. Very early in the conversation, I recognized earnestness rather than resistance in Frieda's demonstration. The customer service department was staffed by women, and each one stopped by while Frieda and I worked and explained her own frustrations in some detail. Yet I could not deny, either, that it appeared each employee had, in the past several months, come to equate their dislike of the new software with their dislike for the merger.

Either the customer service department really, genuinely, believed the software did not work and it was, in their bias, inextricably connected to the recent merger … *or the software really did not work and one reason the merger was producing lackluster results was due to this underperforming software!*

Even Franklin did not deny that the software company itself possessed only a fleeting commitment to customer service. Our own customer service employees continued to sit on hold for hours calling the software company with the most basic questions. And, while our own customer service folks were on calls attempting to get software solutions, our publishing customers were calling unanswered phones. That was affecting our own sales. And profit. And morale.

When an executive who had participated in the decision to buy the software swung by our division on routine corporate business, I made a point of asking about the software. Why had it been purchased? How had the decision to purchase it been made? Was there some way to get better customer service support? His answer stunned me. The man smiled winsomely and shrugged. "Once they sell you the software, they care less about whether you like it!"

"But … does it work?" I asked.

He laughed. "People don't like change," he said.

As I'd sat beside Frieda, who clearly was convinced that the software was unusable, I realized that I wanted her to be wrong. But I just couldn't ignore something she said with absolute conviction. "Do you know when this company started going downhill?" she asked. "About a year after we bought this software!"

Franklin. Franklin's lackluster results. Franklin's software solutions … was there a connection?

Off to finance I trudged. If Viola*, the comptroller, could provide me with a few spreadsheets, I would know whether there was any validity to Frieda's claim. Certainly, Frieda's conviction explained why the software and the merger seemed inextricably linked in the minds of our customer service representatives.

Ideally, I'd take a look and realize that Frieda was well-meaning but wrong.

As I reviewed Viola's spreadsheets, though, I couldn't rule out Frieda's theory. The sales dollars did plunge six months to a year after the software had been purchased and installed—which coincided roughly with the first-year anniversary of the acquisition. As I looked at the numbers more closely, I became even more alarmed. As I reviewed the data, I was seeing dropped accounts. Many, many of them.

I called the corporate executive I'd spoken to the week before and explained what I had found. He grew quite angry. "People don't like change!"

"But how do you know the software works?" I asked.

"It worked during the demonstration!" he snapped.

"Who did the demonstration?" I asked. "Frieda and the team?" Silence. "No," he said finally. "The salesman did the demonstration."

I thanked him, hung up, and walked over to the sales department. I told Frieda that I believed her.

The company never recovered from that software misstep. The cost of new account acquisition at that time was roughly three times the cost of retention. Investing three times what we had lost to woo back the accounts dropped by the flawed software was prohibitive. The revenues of our flagship newsletter* had been reduced by one-third—and nobody had noticed that the software was losing track of accounts until they were gone. *Nobody had listened to Frieda.*

A corporate leader does not herself need to be a technology expert to lead a successful software adoption initiative. Frankly, as important as it is to know what to do, it's just as important to know how *not* to do it. To this day, whenever a software decision must be made, I follow the same process borne of that fiasco so many years ago. Indeed, at The Arc NLC, and now at The Arc ECT, we very carefully—scrupulously, actually—follow the process to this day. This is how we evaluate software and make software purchase decisions:

Essential Criteria for Successful Software Evaluation and Adoption

1. **NETWORK.** Who are your industry's biggest players, not locally but nationally? What software do they use? (If you are the industry

leader, remember this: It's almost always good to be first—but we at The Arc proceed cautiously with all software adoption.) Use your network to gather information.

2. **EVALUATE.** Have a trusted information technology professional explore demo copies of the software options. How is the software engineered and coded? Does the software have design integrity? How does it work structurally, and in terms of outcomes? Determine which programs seem to be the best from a software-design stand-point *as well as* a user-standpoint and an outcomes-standpoint.

3. **GET UP FROM YOUR DESK.** You as the CEO will not have the time to track down the end user of a particular software. Send your IT leader to do it for you, along with a leader of the department that will be using the software. *This is important!* Do not ask another CEO or a manager or a person who might have purchased the software but does not use it herself whether it works! It is essential for your team to meet the end-users of the product. Sit beside them. Ask: Does it work? How does it work? Can you show me? Do you like it? Why or why not? Always keep in mind that a software dealers' salesforce uses the program(s) all the time, and it's the sales crew's job to know it inside and out so they can sell it. Their proficiency in no way translates to the experience your team will have in learning that software.

4. **LEASE DON'T BUY.** When your IT professionals have satisfied themselves that they know the industry standout in terms of software, lease it—don't buy it. The day you buy software is the day, as that executive so nonchalantly noted, that the seller no longer needs to worry about you. Unlike real estate, software becomes obsolete quickly. A single version of software, unlike the house you live in, is never a long-term investment. A software dealer that leases software and contracts to upgrade and maintain it and staff a helpline for it has a built-in economic reason to make sure it works. A dealer that merely sells software does not. Once they have your money, you are yesterday's news. And they are on to the next sale.

5. **TRAIN, TRAIN, TRAIN.** Never sell your team short when it comes to training. When team members feel safe raising a hand and asking for extra help, the right software will pay dividends. At

The Arc, we never shame people who struggle with technology. We reward people who ask for help by providing the help they need. The learning curve for adoption can vary widely. Occasionally, a worker will need to be trained several times, and we are fine with that. People who need a lot more help receive it, and that support goes a long way in preventing a workforce's resistance to new technology adoption—and change in general. Such support, by the way, also builds a lot of trust.

6. **KNOW HOW TO BUY SOFTWARE.** To summarize: Who are the big players? What software do they use? Evaluate options. Get up from your desk—or, more specifically, have your team get up from their desks and, as their leader, coach them how to do so. Do the end users believe the software aids the fulfillment of their job responsibilities and improves results? Again, lease; don't buy. And train, train, train.

The costs of a team's fear of technology cannot be overemphasized. For nearly a decade, The Arc ECT has enjoyed one of the largest IT departments in the field relative to our size. In fact, never have I worked at a for-profit that enjoyed such technological largesse.

Many, many years of frustration watching teams struggle because they lacked the technological tools and support needed to succeed informs our decision to invest, invest, invest in IT. I confess that watching the publishing industry miss the boat on the Internet influences me greatly here also.

Nowhere does investment pay off better, dollar-for-dollar, than with information technology. At The Arc, we also use software for ensuring health and safety—something that cannot be expressed in dollars or cents.

Here is a list of our current technological platforms, uses and costs over the last 12 years. Please note, the following tallies do *not* include the cost of training—which is substantial—but difficult to quantify since the agency takes a benevolent approach to retraining as needed. However, it's important to note that any technology investment is value-less if adequate training support is not provided. So, The Arc ECT continues to train exhaustively and patiently as needed.

Current Technological Platforms		
Payroll HRIS Services-ADP (27.96%)	Computrace (2.08%)	Dash Cams (0.79%)
Copying/Printing (13.04%)	Financial Software (1.67%)	Marketing & Design Software (0.54%)
Computer Equip (11.16%)	Contacts Database (1.36%)	Maintenance Software (0.42%)
eFax (1.30%)	Modems-Remote Internet (7.73%)	Assisted Living Tech (0.39%)
Cell Phones (7.02%)	Microsoft Office (1.25%)	Firewall Software (0.35%)
Therap (6.44%)	Security Equip & Monitoring (1.24%)	Webhosting (0.30%)
GPS Equip & Monitoring (4.90%)	Tablets (1.05%)	Antivirus Software (0.26%)
Time Clock (3.57%)	Relias Training Software (0.96%)	Personnel Records Scanning (0.11%)
VOIP Phone System (3.12%)	Backup Software (0.90%)	Vechicle Key Management (0.07%)
Grand Total: **$3,536,972**	Budget Size: **$149,895,924**	% of Total Budget: **2.36%**

The Arc Eastern Connecticut's technology-investment dollars were realized from merger savings. In turn, the technologies adopted yielded ever greater efficiencies and savings giving the agency a strategic advantage when post-recession budget cuts slammed the state's human service providers.

Why do so many for-profit and nonprofit organizations fail in the software-adoption arena? A poverty of expectation exists almost universally in a variety of ways: Too many for-profits don't want to invest profits in technology because then they will appear, well, less profitable. So, they trade long-term efficiencies for those popular short-term dollars. And too many nonprofits—not just those who serve people with IDD—believe that poverty is a virtue. But one challenge nonprofits eschewing tech adoption will have to explain is why passing up its efficiencies, including software purchases at cut rate prices, can possibly make sense.

In writing this chapter, I sat with Seth, Chief Technology and Design Officer of The Arc ECT. I wanted Seth's perspective on the ways excellence in the nonprofit sector is driven and sustained via IT. His insights are incredibly valuable, and my horizons were expanded by his point of view.

First, Seth explained that nonprofits pay only 25 percent of what for-profits pay for software. To him, a nonprofit's failure to strategically exploit this deep discount remains unfathomable. While I agree, I would add that nonprofit CEOs need to be aware that grants are an important aspect of nonprofit tech adoption. Funders want to invest in pragmatic, progressive nonprofits. Nothing says a nonprofit has its act together better than a well-run, well-stocked IT department. In our experience, it is not too difficult to get funders interested in providing grants for technology and training either.

A culture of excellence demands collaboration between IT and the rest of the team in terms of problem-solving and troubleshooting. Seth sees tech training and communication as essential keys to The Arc ECT's overall success, and he believes The Arc ECT's approach is critical in this regard.

"A lot of organizations start with *what*," Seth explains. "The agencies tell employees what they are going to do tech-wise. We do it differently. We start with the *why*. We explain to people *why we are doing this*, rather than *what we are doing.*

"That's important to the buy-in," he says, "because training is a critical part of The Arc's culture, along with empowerment, since people can't learn if they don't feel comfortable making mistakes or asking questions."

Seth impressed me further by pointing out that shame and tech too often go hand-in-hand when that should never be the case. "That's another reason people avoid tech," he says. "Too many IT departments shame employees. They take the position of 'I know this so I'm smart and you don't, so you're not.'"

"I've had a manager who we had to go over (to their department) three times literally to train one of her team members to turn the computer on." Seth shrugged.

> We could have come at it by saying, "How ridiculous." But we didn't come at it that way. I just talked to the supervisor and said, "Hey, when you're having a conversation with this team member, can you remind so-and-so where the on button is?"
>
> And we got the person up to speed that way. A lot of IT departments also come at it like, "You're stupid for struggling with this." We don't do that. These people have other people's lives in their hands. We need to account for that and help them to do better rather than shame them.

I asked Seth if he could explain why so many organizations—regardless of sector—fail to embrace technology and all its advantages.

"Some of it is dated thinking," he said, "and I don't mean dated thinking by not embracing technology alone. A lot of people just are not aware of the way tech has changed in the last ten years. It used to be every three years you needed to upgrade your hardware. But I just retired a computer that was ten years old. It was perfectly fine. So, a lot of people got into that mindset that if you buy it, then you will have to replace it all every few years. That just isn't true anymore, but people don't know it."

In a similar vein: "Upper management got used to people complaining about how the tech never works," Seth notes. "And they didn't want to deal with that. In other cases, people learned to tolerate bad equipment—because they really had bad equipment—and that doesn't have to be the case either."

I asked Seth to tell me a little more about this, and he said:

People got used to being stuck with the same software for years and years and years [because companies thought they were saving money by not investing in new software]. If the tech is working, and if it's up to date and you're not waiting a half hour to reboot, you actually have people working rather than off talking to other people while *they* reboot. But people still remember waiting forever for their computer to turn on, and that isn't true anymore either.

"It's actually a philosophy," Seth points out. "SaaS, or Software as a Service. It's a computer term, and it refers to security and user ease. It refers to tech infrastructure as a service. This is cloud-based architecture. We use it, and it's called SaaS."

Seth added that he essentially agrees with my advice about leasing and acquiring technology. He pointed out, though, that his own philosophy is rooted in SaaS. "My own experience has exposed me and brought me into the IT-as-a-service philosophy via the SaaS method," he said. While Seth likewise agrees that leasing software rather than buying really is a better idea, SaaS drives his opinion here as well. "Paying a monthly fee," he says, "which is what you do with cloud-based architectures, is more [fiscally] manageable than buying upfront."

Customer service is a key component of SaaS. And it works both ways, serving team members as much as employers. "We have a pool of computers," Seth says. "We can have you up and running in thirty minutes. [If you have a computer problem,] we pull that computer and take it back to the shop [The Arc's main administrative building] to fix it rather than working at your desk."

"That's a big thing with me," he says. "We don't have IT techs in the group homes for five hours fixing the computers. No. Swap it out, bring it home, and work on it there."

I pointed out that this approach is doubly beneficial as a technician in a busy group home not only prevents that home's leadership and team members from using the computer in process of repair there—quite possibly affecting health and safety in areas of medical records, medicine administration, and more—but residents of that group home have the imposition of the tech department in their personal home space.

Seth agreed and said that in office settings, the effect is different but equally problematic. When tech workers fix computers at work sites, disabled computers mean down time for busy team members.

Seth laughed:

And then the employee whose computer is being fixed goes and disturbs another employee who was working because the person with down time has nothing to do while they wait. Plus, the tech is in the way of the job that's supposed to be getting done, which is exactly what we discussed about the group homes.

I asked Seth if he could think of any other reasons for tech reticence and/or resistance within workforces. He thought for a minute and pointed out that he had discussed with another agency's executive director her reason for not wanting computers or Internet service in group homes. "She told me she didn't want people abusing it," he said. "I told her, 'You've got a TV in there ... what's the difference?'"

Seth said the executive simply didn't realize how necessary technology is to modern nonprofits. The agency had extremely slow computers and very old software. "They took forever to use," he says. After a short pause and a laugh, he adds that he once helped out with some IT work at the agency. "There were literally cobwebs in the computers when I opened them to clean them."

He points out that for many businesses, particularly small ones, technology—even now—just isn't seen as a priority. "It's seen as something extra," he says.

What would Seth say to organizational leaders who feel this way? "The Internet, now, is becoming as important as electricity," he said. "The government is viewing it as a utility."

I pointed out that, for The Arc Quinebaug Valley, a retiring executive director and a lack of technology proved a major trigger for a merger. Leadership and IT were immediate needs, and Quinebaug's Board of Directors and retiring executive clearly understood that. Seth nodded.

> They knew they needed tech but didn't know what they needed. They didn't like the attitude of their existing IT service, but they didn't understand how much their own [core] services were affected by not having tech. They didn't know what they needed for IT until they learned about our IT and saw what it was doing for us.

It's not surprising that a professional like Seth would be quick to embrace technology. But he pointed out that chief executives can't afford to avoid it either. "Our time clocks allow us to limit overtime," he said, "and to ensure actual time worked. The vehicle GPS units allow us to monitor speed and location. Our cameras prevent theft, accidents and encourage accountability."

Since we know that transformation has to happen across platforms to really "stick," then what Seth says about IT taking a customer-centric approach makes even more sense. If an agency mostly embraces virtue, training, transformation, and excellence, then just one lagging department will jeopardize the progress of the whole organization and the whole strategic plan. One department, all by itself, can become a roadblock to the attainment of excellence of the whole organization.

Think about it this way: Let's say you commit to IT but your human resources department continues to hire tech-averse team members and refuses to embrace online recruiting. Onboarded team members will be more likely to be tech averse and therefore resistant to embracing a tech-rich status quo. Team members are walking in the door, then, already set up to struggle. And, as Seth notes, if IT workers take a holier-than-thou approach to computer support, team members with real tech needs will indeed dread making a call for help. Concrete examples of transformative excellence can be hard to illustrate, but this is one place where we can readily see why a seamless mission, implemented across all operational platforms (Think Adapted McKinsey 7S ... "*My Transformation Plan*"), is necessary for driving transformative excellence.

Beyond that, as a former journalist, it's important to note that The Arc and nonprofits like it provide a host of taxpayer subsidized services. Thanks to a wide range of technologies, from case notes to time clocks to vehicle key tracking—every move we make, every day, is recorded and accounted for. That alone fosters efficiency and quality of service. It also fosters accountability. And isn't that the stuff of excellence?

The Secrets of Chapter 9

- TECHNOLOGY IS NO LONGER A PERK. From efficiency to health and safety to team and customer satisfaction—technology is no less a utility than electricity.
- INVEST IN A SUPERPOWER: TECH. From team training to service innovations, technology helps companies do more in more customized, smarter ways.
- A POVERTY OF EXPECTATION LIMITS TECH AND ALL IT CAN DO FOR YOU. Cross-sector, misconceptions about how technology really works, its real costs, and what it can do prevent desperately needed innovation. Misconceptions also limit your ability to identify strategic solutions to challenges that hold potential within them—boosting your mission, quest for excellence, and bottom line.

For Discussion

- WHERE SHOULD YOU BE INVESTING? What are your troublesome cost-centers? Overtime? High gasoline costs? Theft? How would you like to see things change? **Make a list of efficiencies and goals that might be served via tech solutions. Don't forget to invest in and enlist your team in building the enthusiasm needed to embrace progress.**
- DO YOU HARBOR MISCONCEPTIONS. Did anything you read in this chapter surprise you? What? Why? How might this be limiting your mission and your ability to achieve excellence? What has to change?

CHAPTER 10

Influence Public Opinion to Get Results

While it's not difficult to understand why transformation requires cross-operational implementation for consistency and excellence to prevail, working internally presents one type of challenge. Influencing external forces poses quite another. Successful CEOs need to navigate both with proficiency.

Although I was myself a newcomer to the field, by 2010, the successive years of flat funding and budget cuts that Connecticut had handed its private, largely nonprofit, social service provider network was an established concern statewide. Years of neglect were shredding the state's human services safety net. Although the pre-Recession years had at times delivered significant budget surpluses in the state, Connecticut had chosen to invest in its own publicly run human services network even as other states had begun to dismantle theirs in favor of nonprofit service contractors.

The motivation among those states that did move to outsource human services to nonprofit contractors was nimbleness and efficiency. Doing so enabled states to free their budgets (and taxpayers) from the costs of administrative infrastructure and pensions and health care as well as the brick-and-mortar expenses that armies of state-employed human service workers necessitated. But even as most states opted for private-sector safety nets administered and monitored by streamlined state workforces, Connecticut did the opposite. Bucking national administrative and economic trends is one thing: Connecticut's real mistake was failing to create a plan for funding the considerably more expensive path it had chosen.

As world and national economies grew distressed, Connecticut's budget deficit ballooned.

While America staggered through the Great Recession, Connecticut haplessly thrashed its way through negative headlines screaming about its skyrocketing public sector costs, especially its woefully underfunded state employee pension debt (Phaneuf 2019).

The state's wobbly economy notwithstanding, I had specific concerns in those days for The Arc NLC itself. Eastern Connecticut had always struggled economically to keep pace with the financially infused west, fueled by well-to-do towns like hedge-fund rich Greenwich. Despite Connecticut's standing as one of the wealthiest states in the country, its western affluence—year after year—failed to flow eastward. Despite the diligence of Eastern Connecticut's elected leaders, fewer voters and rural dollars left the eastern half of the state feeling ignored, overlooked, and disenfranchised. Even when there was largesse to go around, our half of the state felt a bit like the poor relations of fairy tale fare.

Host to the U.S. Navy's first submarine base, defense contractor General Dynamics and, at one time, world headquarters for Pfizer, Southeastern Connecticut looked on as successive waves of industrial downsizing and government defense cuts hit the region harder and harder. Efforts to stave off the effects of the economic downturn had begun in the 1990s, but the Great Recession still slammed our region harder than most. Consequently, even as the Recession receded elsewhere, Eastern Connecticut continued to stumble. For a time, Southeastern Connecticut, specifically New London County, held the unwelcome distinction of being among the 10 worst economies in the nation post-Recession (Brooks 2015).

Though economic circumstances have improved dramatically for Eastern Connecticut since then, the advocacy tactics outlined in this chapter are one reason the area's prospects took a turn for the better. Responsive civic leaders, voters, and legislators, in bipartisan fashion, deserve credit for ultimately hearing and responding to the message, which itself was crafted in desperation.

But before that happened, by the end of the Recession in 2009, the human service needs of economically battered Southeastern Connecticut had mushroomed so sharply that health and human safety providers in the region struggled in the face of the crushing demand. The need for reduced and free school lunches for children, for example, rose 14.8 percent more than elsewhere in the state. Likely reflecting the greater economic stress on households and families in the area, domestic violence increased 8.9 percent while decreasing everywhere else in Connecticut. The bottom line for Southeast Connecticut's nonprofit health and human service providers was that, from 2006 through 2011, *their revenues dropped by an average of 18 percent* even while the area's frugal agencies *served measurably heavier* caseloads than peers statewide. The region's health and human service workforce, meantime, was and remains predominantly women and people of color (Stanley McMillen 2014).

Such was the economic environment I walked into upon arriving at The Arc NLC in 2009. Our direct support professionals and loyal agency leadership and their families were gasping from years of flat wages, overwork, and the stress of delivering chronically underfunded services to chronically distressed residents.

For years, nonprofit health and human service providers had been making the hour-plus ride from the shoreline up to Hartford with their tales of woe. Every year, it was a refrain: "*We are doing more with less.*" Legislators listened politely and thanked everybody for "doing God's work" and having lots of "passion." Unfortunately, changing the status quo would "cost too much." So, nothing changed.

As statistics would ultimately prove via the Nonprofit Economic Impact Study funded and sponsored in 2014 by The Arc NLC, the Community Foundation of Eastern Connecticut, United Way of Southeastern Connecticut, the Chamber of Commerce, the Southeastern Connecticut Cultural Coalition and key local human service providers including Child and Family Agency and Thames Valley Council for Community Action (TVCCA), nonprofit human service executives had been telling their legislators in Hartford the truth. Increasingly, Connecticut's nonprofit human service providers were serving more and more people with fewer and fewer resources. While efficiency is a wonderful thing, starvation is another matter.

The Arc and its overworked, overstressed workforce were making do by hiring part-time employees because Connecticut's contract payments to the agency no longer were sufficient to cover the cost of the basic health care insurance that full-time employees would have required. To the extent that we, the state's nonprofit executive leaders, were failing to wrest fair wages and benefits out of our legislature and governor for our workforce, we were failing our teams. Murray was worrying aloud about how to afford the skyrocketing costs of health care for our dwindling full-time team as we received new (and much higher) insurance quotes each Fall. I knew it wasn't about the money for Murray. He hated what the cuts were doing to our team members' households' bottom lines. Like Murray, I worried, too.

> Though economic circumstances have improved dramatically for Eastern Connecticut since then, the advocacy tactics outlined in this chapter are one reason the area's prospects took a turn for the better. Responsive civic leaders, voters, and legislators, in bipartisan fashion, deserve credit for ultimately hearing and responding to the message, which was itself crafted in desperation.

Around my six-month anniversary at The Arc, one of the agency's executive board members, Rick DeMatto, asked during our regular monthly board meeting what worried me the most about the coming years. Finding money for raises and retaining talent, I told him. And, surviving. **"After years of Recession, Connecticut's tax base will need years to recover," I told our Board. "Given past trends, that means significant funding *cuts* lie ahead, even after all these years of flat funding and budget reductions. Contract revenues do not always cover real costs as it is. With cuts, we will be fighting for survival."**

I remembered Franklin shouting at the team until his nose bled. Now, I felt irritation at how, as our organization's leader, he had blamed us and taken no personal responsibility for our straits. *What do you do when no one knows what to do?* The words of Harvard's Dutch Leonard bear repeating.

Past chapters outline a host of actions Franklin could have, but did not, take. Among them: Invest in the best team you can find. Strategize. Improvise. Decide to thrive even if you don't yet have answers to all the questions at hand. Take an inventory of your challenges and solutions—cross-operationally—and then address each one; next, brainstorm tactics for advancing those solutions and strategies. Make sure your team has as many resources as you can muster, and then lead and encourage your team to keep moving forward. Create and maintain an environment of respect, cooperation, and accountability so team leaders and team members can support and affirm one another.

Amid great economic uncertainty and external stress, that is exactly what The Arc NLC did from 2009 right through the pandemic. Resigning oneself to a difficult reality doesn't mean you have to do it quietly, though.

Even in the post-Recession climate, as private sector businesses began hiring and wages began rising again, nobody wanted to hear that human service professionals deserved raises too—not the state legislators grappling daily with deep budget woes, not the governor, and certainly not taxpayers. Not surprisingly, as private sector wages increased, finding direct support professionals to fill human service jobs, with their low wages, part-time hours, and elusive benefits, only got harder.

Increasingly, amid shifting political winds, Connecticut voters were indicating that they didn't want to pay for human services at all. "We like supporting The Arc," one local funder told me, "The people you serve [people with Intellectual Disability] didn't ask for their misfortune. They didn't create their own problems because they were born that way."

The sentiment alarmed me. All around, I witnessed colleagues leading nonprofit agencies, doing great good in the world by helping people get sober, return to productive lives and jobs and, yes, rejoin the workaday world as taxpayers. Parents were taught parenting skills so their children might grow up functional and productive. Homeless families received a safe place to sleep with rapid rehousing supports to prevent employment loss. And I'd learned that, contrary to popular belief, almost half of all homeless people actually do hold jobs (National Coalition for the Homeless 2009).

Coming from a for-profit background, everywhere I looked, I saw proof that investing in human beings makes good economic sense. Perhaps we human service providers needed to find a new way to communicate the facts amid a fragile, post-Recession economy. Showing the good we did via newspaper articles and storytelling, only a lukewarm antidote to budget cuts in good times, certainly wasn't going to work now. The prevailing sentiment in Connecticut at that time was that increasing human service funding was sheer folly, a politically impossible and ill-advised task.

But we, Connecticut's human services leaders, needed to deal with the very real problem we had: Not only were Southeastern Connecticut's human service nonprofits at their breaking point, doing more and more with less and less, but the people we employed were increasingly falling into the category of the "working poor," hard-working people with multiple jobs, no health care benefits, and wages too to scant to cover the high cost of living in our beautiful yet expensive state.

Ironically, by underfunding its nonprofit contractors, Connecticut had inadvertently added to its own human service burdens as many of our direct support professionals, despite their hardworking habits and multiple jobs, needed assistance themselves. Taxpayers and legislators alike needed to be educated on the economics driving the value of human service investment.

As the person who in those days signed the checks at The Arc NLC, I wondered if the donor who saw human services as a hand-out understood how many local businesses we supported—including her own employer. Fortunately, I was not alone. One Sunday morning, I picked up *The Day* newspaper and read an article quoting the executive director of a local arts organization on the role that the local arts scene played in helping make the Connecticut shoreline a tourist destination. The arts in our region, the article explained, indirectly brought tourist dollars to local businesses and to our local economy.

The next day, I picked up the phone and called Wendy Bury of the Southeastern Connecticut Cultural Coalition. I liked what she'd said in *The Day*, I told her. Would she work with The Arc NLC to put a study together to show the positive economic impact of all the nonprofits in our region? Bury didn't hesitate. She would gladly work on finding an economist to do such study, she replied, but I would need to help fund it.

Several phone calls later, we had $7,000 for a nonprofit economic impact study to measure the value of the investment that Connecticut's nonprofit dollars posed to Southeastern Connecticut's for-profit businesses. The Eastern Connecticut Chamber of Commerce, The Community Foundation, United Way, and two of the region's largest nonprofits readily agreed to put up the dollars needed to fund the study.

It took about a year, but in 2014, Bury, our funding partners, and The Arc NLC together commissioned University of Connecticut economist

Stanley McMillen to produce: *The Economic, Fiscal, and Social Impacts of Health and Human Services Public Charities in New London Connecticut.*

The report would alter public perceptions of human service provision by proving how dramatically nonprofit human service investment benefits local businesses and local economies. Just as important, it eased the standoff between the state of Connecticut and its nonprofit contractors by reframing the traditional debate surrounding human service spending.

In fact, our study revealed that nonprofits contributed more than $1 billion *per year, each year,* to businesses in New London County from 2005 to 2010 alone; additionally, nonprofits paid $35 million in indirect taxes while our employees themselves paid another $16 million directly to the state and to local municipalities. One-hundred-and-fifty nonprofits provided 7 percent of the region's jobs, and nonprofit entities poured $560 million in wages into Southeastern Connecticut's towns. The Arc NLC alone, with some $13 million in revenues, spent $100,000 on gasoline and vehicles and maintenance; $47,000 more in fuel oil; and another $50,000 in office supplies; we spent $129,000 more buying group home groceries. And that was just a snapshot (McMillen 2014).

We took our study on a speaking tour, talking to Chamber of Commerce audiences, legislators, then-lieutenant governor Nancy Wyman, and even Connecticut's state budget director at the time, Ben Barnes, who so loved our data that he quizzed Murray and me and State Senator Paul Formica, a local representative and member of The Arc ECT's Board, who accompanied us, for an hour-and-a-half. The analysis definitively proved that an investment in nonprofits on the part of state government and taxpayers was an investment in local businesses.

Republican legislators who previously had seen human services as an economic drain changed their views almost overnight, openly challenging the state's Democratic governor about whether ongoing human service cuts would harm the small businesses in their districts. I knew we had made meaningful progress when local business owners began to approach us to ask if we could partner somehow. Convinced that doing business with nonprofits was a win for themselves, for the community and for people in need, the community's for-profit businesses readily embraced the kinds of partnerships that lie at the heart of every strong community.

Many of these business owners had long supported us, and we believed strongly in buying local anyway. Now, we doubled down to support them, and they did the same for us.

When the Republican party in Connecticut proposed an alternative to democratic Governor Dannel Malloy's unpopular 2015 budget (even many democratic state legislators didn't like it), I was invited along with some colleagues to consult with the minority party's budget committee. *The result? The Connecticut Republican Party proposed to increase human service spending statewide via the private provider network as a support to both our communities and our businesses.* At long last, investing in human beings had begun to make good economic sense in Connecticut.

As I'd stood outside the velvet ropes designating the meeting rooms of the Republican party in the Connecticut State Capitol prior to the budget caucus, a nattily attired Hartford policy maker had sidled up. "What are *you* doing here?" he asked. "I've been invited," I answered cheerily. He frowned. I smiled. No more groveling for the nonprofits of New London County. The people we serve have value, our work has value, and we'd finally proven it.

This is how Southeastern Connecticut's regional nonprofits became a recognized resource for media and for legislators seeking to quantify the economic value of human services investment in Connecticut. Despite the severe economic challenges facing the state, the year-after-year budget slashing of nonprofit service providers finally was halted. More important, the effort to avoid human service cuts quickly became bipartisan, even as national politics grew more divisive. Indeed, Connecticut's residents today benefit greatly from the ability of their state legislators to work unselfishly across the aisle. It's a habit we can't afford to lose. And it's an example the nation would do well to follow.

Board members at The Arc Quinebaug Valley, in the northeast corner of Connecticut, took note of this success when their executive director expressed an interest in retiring. In approaching The Arc NLC to discuss possible partnership opportunities, they cited the nonprofit economic impact study and The Arc NLC's growing influence in steering public opinion as being among the reasons for their interest in joining forces. (Our knowledge of and effective use of technology, as noted, was another.) Quinebaug's directors wanted that kind of clout in Hartford for the people they served and for their workforce, too.

Affiliated chapters of The Arc in other states around the country began inquiring how they might commission nonprofit economic impact studies.

Emboldened by the economic impact the state's human service agencies were obviously making in local economies, and now able to demonstrate it statistically, Connecticut's nonprofits began approaching political candidates for the state legislature and governor's offices. Why not provide a higher minimum wage for human services professionals, we asked? Connecticut could set an example for the nation and use the higher wage as a kind of economic stimulus within its boundaries by putting more money into local economies via higher wages for frontline workers', or direct support professionals', wages. Because we had educated our audience well, it was clear that candidates—and even sitting legislators—were warming to the idea of a higher minimum wage for DSPs. Yet, understandably, state leaders also were worried about what voters (read taxpayers) would think.

We had done a lot to educate the public, but clearly, we needed to do more. I could hear Frank Connolly, a public administration professor from my graduate school years, speaking to our class: "Give the mayor the tools he needs to do what he wants to do." Frank had served so many cities and towns throughout Connecticut so well that he was something of a legend among municipal officials and among his graduate students too. It was Frank who had taught me that public officials usually want to advance social change; but they need to know they have the votes to do it.

Connecticut's nonprofits had, for too long, failed to grasp that we had our own army of voters within our own ranks and within our own service perimeters. We began educating our workforce and our constituents and encouraging them to hit the polls. We were also learning that approaching lawmakers with blueprints and prescriptions for problem-solving rather than approaching them with endless complaints and headaches greatly improved our chances of getting representatives to sign on to our causes.

If we were asking our legislators to go out on a limb, then we needed to meet them halfway. After examining tactics of various advocacy groups, and with the help of other chapters of The Arc in the state, the teams of The Arc NLC and The Arc Connecticut designed a Voter Guide. This made it easier for legislators to support a fair shake for people with IDD and their families; it made it easier for lawmakers to support a higher minimum wage for direct support professionals, in this case, about $4 more than the state's existing minimum wage. In hopes of stabilizing their staffing needs, families signed on to support better pay for the workforce that supported their kids and loved ones. *Legislators and voters became better informed together.*

The Voter Guide is popular among our advocates, their families, our team members, and state legislators alike because it concisely outlines the relevant issues at stake. Representatives who support people with IDD and their families, their civil rights, and direct support professionals' right to fair wages like it also because speaking clearly on issues translates into votes.

The Arcs of Connecticut have managed to effectively quantify our audience. For example, The Arc ECT can offer supportive legislators in its district a potential bloc of some 3,000 to 4,000 votes, a sphere of influence encompassing people with IDD, their families, their guardians, The Arc's team of employees and their families as well. Each Connecticut affiliate of The Arc does the same. The Arc ECT (and the rest of the state's affiliated chapters) aggressively promote voting as a civic duty. Particularly given the rural, low-density demographics of Eastern Connecticut—where candidate races can be won and lost on very slim margins—our votes matter.

The Voter Guide is essentially a four-page pamphlet. *The cover frames the issue of the year such as: 2020 Vote! Protect services, jobs, and our safety net!* Evolving each year based on the issues at hand and subject to state and federal lobby regulations, the inside pages outline and explain the bills and issues likely to be put to a vote in the coming legislative session as well as candidates' voting records. The back page of the pamphlet outlines voter rights, how to register to vote, how to get to the polls and how to find your polling place:

The Arc movement in America's driving motivation has always been mission. That mission, for The Arc ECT, remains: "In Partnership for Full Equality." In America, you don't always need money to build influence and clout. The Arc is a grassroots organization, and The Arc and nonprofits like it are what grassroots organizing in a democracy is all about.

ELECTION 2☑20

Voting During the Pandemic

Be aware of your voting options
—*Exercise your right to vote*

This year, due to the COVID-19 pandemic, all voters in Connecticut are eligible to vote by absentee ballot or in person in the general election, held on November 3, 2020. *It's your choice to do what's best and safest for you and your family.*

MAKE SURE YOU ARE REGISTERED TO VOTE:

- Check the Secretary of the State's website: portal.ct.gov/sots
- The deadline to register to vote online, by postmarked mail, and in person is Tuesday, October 27, 2020.

ABSENTEE BALLOT VOTING

Did you know that the biggest reason that absentee ballots are rejected is that they have not been filled out completely or correctly!

- Applications for absentee ballots will be sent to all registered voters starting in September. If you need one, contact your Town Clerk NOW. Fill it out and get it submitted ASAP.
- Beginning the first week in October, absentee ballots will be sent out. When you get your ballot, fill it out completely and put it in the Official Ballot Drop Box outside of your town hall. You can also mail in your ballot.
- Only complete absentee ballots received before the close of polls on the day of the election will be counted.

VOTING IN PERSON

- Polls are open on November 3, 2020 from 6:00 am - 8:00 pm.
- Locate your polling place: portaldir.ct.gov/sots/LookUp.aspx.
- Need a ride? Contact your Town Clerk to get the numbers for committees in your town offering rides to the polls.

VOTING IS ALWAYS IMPORTANT,
but voting now, during the pandemic, is more important than ever.

ELECTION 2☑20

VOTER'S GUIDE

The Arc.
Eastern Connecticut
TheArcECT.org

The Arc.
Connecticut
TheArcCT.org

We must vote to protect essential services, jobs, and our safety net!

★ ★ ★ ★ ★ ★ ★ ★ ★ ★ ★ ★ ★ ★ ★ ★ ★ ★ ★

OUR VOICES CREATE
POWERFUL
PARTNERSHIPS! ☑

The Arc is Connecticut's oldest and largest community-based organization, serving and advocating for and with people with intellectual and developmental disabilities (IDD) and their families. We are affiliated with The Arc of the United States, the oldest and largest charity federation in the nation dedicated to the same mission. In Connecticut, our 14 local chapters of The Arc deliver over $100 million in jobs and supports to thousands of people in 162 communities. Together, The Arcs are the largest provider of supports and services for people with IDD and their families in the state.

THE ARC CONNECTICUT 2020 CANDIDATE PLEDGE

1. If elected I pledge to protect the civil rights of people with disabilities by supporting legislation to ensure they receive reasonable accommodations in hospitals and other healthcare facilities.
2. If elected I pledge to support legislation that will stabilize the community non-profit system and ensure the highest standards of supports and safety for people with IDD.
3. If elected I pledge to protect the rights of all people with IDD to live and receive supports in their communities.

To learn more about the pledge and to which candidates signed visit:

TheArcCT.org/2020pledgeresults

The Arc 2020 Candidate Pledge was sent to all candidates for the Connecticut General Assembly and Town Chairs, who provided the Secretary of the State with a valid email address.

(Highlighted names on your checklist indicate those candidates who have signed the pledge!)

DESIGN BY:

RECENT CONNECTICUT LEGISLATION SUPPORTING PEOPLE WITH DISABILITIES

To see how currently elected officials voted on the following bills, visit the links provided. *Please note that current candidates who were not already in office did not have an opportunity to vote on these bills.*

To read a bill in its entirety, and to see how the House and Senate voted, using the Quick Bill Search at cga.ct.gov. Enter the calendar year 2019 and the bill number.

Special Act 19-12 AN ACT ESTABLISHING A TASK FORCE TO INCREASE EMPLOYMENT OPPORTUNITIES FOR PERSONS WITH DISABILITIES (#7093) *(Establishes a task force to study increasing employment opportunities for persons with disabilities and to establish financial incentives for businesses that employ persons with disabilities.)*

House Vote *(Click Here)*   Senate Vote *(Click Here)*

Public Act No. 19-49 AN ACT CONCERNING TRANSITIONAL SERVICES FOR CHILDREN WITH AUTISM SPECTRUM DISORDER (#7168) *(Ensures that school age children with autism spectrum disorder receive services from the Department of Developmental Services and are eligible for Medicaid coverage despite family earnings.)*

House Vote *(Click Here)*   Senate Vote *(Click Here)*

Public Act No. 19-184 AN ACT CONCERNING THE PROVISION OF SPECIAL EDUCATION (#7353) *(Protects teachers who make recommendations on behalf of students in PPT meetings; establishes a working group to study services needs in the gap between Birth to 3 and kindergarten; and requires a communication plan for alerting students who are deaf, hard of hearing or both blind or visually impaired and deaf of an emergency situation.)*

House Vote *(Click Here)*   Senate Vote *(Click Here)*

Be an informed voter! Check out: Vote411.org
— a one stop shop for all voting matters

Electronic (or digital) copies of this guide contain active links

While lobbying dollars and their special interests are an increasingly concerning and even alarming aspect of our U.S. democracy, grassroots coalition building still can be very effective: Build influence by cultivating relationships with your Chambers of Commerce, your local Rotary Clubs, and other civic organizations; your local towns and municipalities and mayors and select persons and city councils; with your state legislators and representatives and federal senators and congressional representatives. Make friends with your Governor, regardless of party. Build relationships with local businesses and with your community banks. Build relationships with good will and with votes and with business loyalty. Always, lead with a gift not an ask.

Growing the mission, vision, brand, and influence of an organization, be it nonprofit or for-profit, is at the heart of a CEO's responsibilities. First and foremost, excellent leaders look out for the people they serve and for the folks who serve them—the team. Excellent leaders look out for their towns and their communities. They look out for their boards of directors and their agency's reputation and mission and bottom line. Excellent CEOs never make excuses.

Not surprisingly, when it stopped balancing its budget on the backs of its human services employees, Connecticut began to climb out of its downward economic spiral. A poverty of expectation can prevent organizations from achieving excellence, and it can prevent states and nations from achieving excellence too.

The Secrets of Chapter 10

- BE HONEST WITH YOURSELF. If a crisis lies ahead, assess it cleanly and outline the best possible outcome. Then, focus not on the difficulty of the task(s) at hand, or what solving it might cost; rather, focus on what resources you will need and the specific steps you will have to take to achieve the necessary outcome(s).

- ACQUIRE THE INFORMATION YOU NEED TO OVERCOME THE CHALLENGES AT HAND. What data is required to support your position? Who has the information? What will it take to obtain it? Make lists of sources you need to tap, the data you need to have in hand for solid decision making, and the studies you might cite or create to get the information and results you require.

- LEAD WITH A GIFT. Whether it is respect, goodwill, votes, or community progress—seek to contribute more than you take, give more than you ask. Your agency's mission and your founders' desire to make the world a better place deserve no less.

For Discussion

- WHAT DO YOU DO WHEN EVERYONE SAYS: "THAT'S IMPOSSIBLE!" Decide to thrive, to be excellent, even if you don't yet have all the answers to the problems that need to be addressed. Educate yourself about the challenges you face. Make sure your team has as many resources as you can secure for them, and then encourage your team to keep improvising and to keep moving forward. Provide moral support and encouragement, too—not just "stuff."
- BUILD COALITIONS. Who are your allies? Who are your mentors? How can you bring advantage to them if they join your cause? Too often nonprofits lead with an ask. Far better to lead with a gift. For The Arc ECT, that gift often is a simple $5 bag of cookies. Joy, the delight that can be found in just one cookie and the love that went into making it, can wield far more power than cash.
- GROW YOUR INFLUENCE. What challenge(s) must be met so your organization might thrive, attain, and maintain excellence? What steps must be taken for your agency to assume a community leadership role—along with a statewide or, even, a national role— in meeting those challenges even while you expand your mission, brand, and influence? What resources do you need to do that? Make a list of resources required and action steps to be taken. You can do it!

CHAPTER 11

Is Bigger Always Better?

Walking into the board room that Tuesday evening in 2013, I felt pretty good. The Arc NLC was becoming, thanks to our talented team, a non-profit transformational phenomenon. Having completed our merger with Seacorp, Inc., (Emma's family-founded agency), The Arc NLC was now posting greatly improved quality service scores, the qualitative measurement of service delivery outcomes from our contracted funder, the state of Connecticut. In fact, outcomes had improved 8 to 12 percent across the board in just two years (Department of Developmental Services 2009).

This meant The Arc's overall quality service scores had reached 97 to 100 percent across all delivery sectors. Our marketing team, via branded, creative, attractive brochures and via the media, had a lively community buzz going. Less and less, people asked, "What is The Arc and what does it do?"

Community demand for our services had grown robust. Thanks to The Arc NLC/Seacorp, Inc. merger, The Arc NLC had grown from a $5.5 million agency to a $9+ million agency, nearly doubling in size in just two years despite the funding squalls and storms marking the Great Recession and its aftermath.

In 2013 alone, The Arc NLC would post another $1.7 million in revenue growth, closing the year as a $10.8 million agency (Stauffer 2014). One legislator, in touring its facilities, declared The Arc NLC/Seacorp, Inc., merger: "The Gold Standard by which all other nonprofit mergers should be measured."

A case has been made that excellent mergers reap excellent results along with measurable, positive outcomes. Here, specifically, is how the merger transformed The Arc NLC and Seacorp into a stronger, better nonprofit to the benefit of the Southeastern Connecticut community.

How Merger Can Ensure Stronger Outcomes

- **TRAINING and QUALITY.** In joining forces with Seacorp, The Arc NLC put Emma in charge of training and quality, and she delivered—revamping training, reorganizing teams, establishing quality baselines, and more.
- **TECH, TALENT, and INFRASTRUCTURE INVESTMENT.** Administrative savings achieved by combining functions such as finance, payroll, and quality allowed for investments in technology and talent, which led to a growth spurt for the newly formed agency d.b.a. (doing business as) The Arc NLC.
- **EFFICIENCY.** The Arc NLC's technology investment far outpaced that of nonprofit agencies of similar size. By tracking costs in ways that other agencies could not, The Arc rolled out a highly efficient, high quality, low-cost service delivery system. (Six years later, The Arc NLC/Quinebaug merger would add another $264,000 in annualized savings in year one of the merger alone. Again, these revenues would facilitate further tech, talent, and quality investments.)
- **GRANTS.** The larger budget enjoyed by the agency now sustained a full-time grant writer. Grant monies began to flow into the agency for critical needs. Vans, health, and safety equipment—and even a lovely patio for participants, team members, and folks in the neighborhood to enjoy—all enhanced the bottom line and mood and motivation of the agency.
- **MORALE.** Annual surpluses, thanks to the new efficiencies, allowed for various team incentives. Rewarding better performance created positive momentum toward even greater outcomes and excellence. The Arc's gains proved exponential as team members who worked at other IDD service providers saw firsthand the contrasts and readily acknowledged them. This, in turn, reinforced trust. It also led to a pioneering spirit toward technology adoption among team members.

And so, I walked into the board room of The Arc NLC that Tuesday evening in 2013 with high spirits given the agency's prospects, our team's successes, and all we had accomplished. The numbers spoke for themselves. We were gaining momentum as quality, technology, and optimism coalesced propelling us to ever greater planes of actualized excellence.

That is, in fact, what I told the board of directors that night. The mood in the room was upbeat as everyone dug into grinders and salads. The Arc ECT always provides simple and nutritious snacks at our in-person board meetings and events. We do the same for team meetings. The best nonprofits invest in their greatest asset: people.

I explain it this way, "Nonprofit" does not mean "poor"; rather, non-profit refers to the essence of The Arc's organizational mission. Nonprofits advance the community good in ways that build and sustain communities, and their primary goal is positive outcomes rather than profit.

Breaking bread is an inherently communal activity valued by societies dating back to biblical times and beyond. Healthy, simple food sustains us, keeps spirits high, allows teams to focus without the distraction of hunger. It graciously yet modestly acknowledges people's efforts on behalf of our mission and the people we serve.

As board members settled in around the table and made small talk, I noticed board president Arthur Stanton* looking pensive. Arthur had a family member with IDD, which made his opinion and input particularly valuable. The work of The Arc lay close to his heart, and he took his responsibilities seriously; indeed, Arthur took most things seriously.

Arthur was unfailingly kind, and his manners had a winsome and gentlemanly refinement, but he could be intense too. An executive-level project manager* by trade, he was detail-oriented and sometimes tried people's patience as the clock wound down and others were looking to wind up a long and productive meeting.

To be honest, Arthur sometimes made me uneasy because I never knew where he might go with his musings. In a positive exercise that successful CEOs sometimes need to learn, I had trained myself to hear Arthur out. Because he might be diverging in a direction I was struggling to follow or didn't want to go was no excuse. Arthur's job as board president charged him with ensuring that we'd considered every angle. To his credit, he did so thoroughly and in ways I ended up finding invaluable.

I had learned a great deal from Arthur even if I'd had to discipline myself to walk paths with him to destinations that weren't readily clear to me.

Now, still looking pensive, Arthur called the meeting to order. Characteristically, he moved methodically through all the formalities his role required: Approval of the minutes for the month prior and then, one by one, each agenda item.

Now it was time for my monthly report, and I began where we had left off as everybody had drifted into the board room and picked up sandwiches and drinks. The Arc NLC's quest for excellence had thus far transformed it into a quality-driven nonprofit approaching $11 million in annual revenues. In three years, we had attracted new talent, revamped training, introduced a host of technologies, reorganized the team, expanded our grant-funding in exponential fashion and steadily grown mission and community influence. I could feel the affirmation in the room, and it felt good. A few people had questions, but they were softballs.

Then, Arthur cleared his throat. "How big," he asked, "is too big?"

To my chagrin, the comment caught on. In minutes the room had begun to buzz like a small beehive as board members began looking at one another, musing: *"How big is too big?"* I managed to stammer out a polite, vague response about results speaking for themselves and thanked Arthur for the question. I told the board they had given me food for thought. Somehow, I got through the meeting and made my way to my vehicle in the dark parking lot. Not only had Arthur kind of stomped on what I felt was our greatest triumph, he'd also mentioned at the meeting's end that a few lights outside the building were burned out. As if getting larger somehow prevented us from buying light bulbs and maintaining safely lit premises! That was Arthur, all about the details.

All the way home, I stewed. "How big is too big? *How big is too big?"* At one point, I got so mad that I shouted at the windshield. "How BIG is TOO big dammit …?!" I really was steamed. *What had I been thinking taking a job at a nonprofit agency?* For all his faults, Franklin never, *ever* questioned profit—let alone an increase of $4 million. Of course, Franklin's leadership never produced that kind of profit, but still.... "Only in nonprofit land," I fumed, "is profit not a good thing!"

It is not uncommon for grassroots organizations to get larger and, in the process, lose sight of the reason they were created.

Arthur's observations had a way of sticking in my craw. During my call-back job interview, Arthur had made it clear he wasn't so sure a for-profit executive was a good fit for The Arc's mom-and pop-operation. "How long is it going to take you to learn the job?" he asked. "Ten years? We don't have ten years!" That night, I'd driven home equally steamed, having lamely responded to the group that I enjoyed learning; I liked to think I learned quickly; and I liked to work hard. I'd also reminded the hiring committee, as respectfully as I could, "I didn't call you guys … you called me.…"

Once home postjob interview, however, I'd got to thinking about what Arthur had said, and the next day I wrote him a personal note. I had intended to thank each person on the interview committee with a handwritten note anyway, but when the time came to write the messages, I handled Arthur's card differently. As with the other notes, I expressed gratitude for the interview. Then, I thanked Arthur for making me think more deeply about why I wanted the job.

I noted that the Great Recession likely meant tough times lay ahead, and if I was correct, my fiscal analysis and budgeting skills could prove important for The Arc's mission and well-being. I noted that, in calling me for the interview, the board had indicated they did not expect I'd be bringing IDD service delivery skills to the table; rather, they were looking for business acumen. I assured Arthur, however, that my years of operational executive experience nevertheless placed me competitively for bringing talent in the door as needed.

Now, having arrived home three years later in a state of similar, indeed somewhat enhanced, irritability I poured a shot of bourbon into a glass, dropped four ice cubes into it, and slunk to a chair. Some of my irritation was rooted in an incontrovertibly annoying reality: No matter how much I wanted to ignore Arthur, I never could.

After my initial hypersensitivity, his words would play through my head. I would then begin pondering them. Before I knew it, I was thinking about things differently, looking at things in a new way. Like it or not,

Arthur exemplifies the quintessential nonprofit board member. Arthur is never harsh, threatening, or unfair. He never makes it personal. He just keeps asking questions, questions for which he himself doesn't necessarily have answers either. *How big is too big?* Now I had begun to wonder too. I was beginning to find Arthur's question … fascinating.

It is not uncommon for grassroots organizations to get larger and, in the process, lose sight of the reason they were created. Covenant House, in New York City, for example, saw its founder, Fr. Bruce Ritter, resign under a cloud of accusations involving the sexual exploitation of minors. More often, though, it's not a national or even a local scandal or horror but the gritty details that derail nonprofits: lack of business expertise in a beloved but obsolete executive; an inattentive board of directors; failure to think strategically or do the hard work of strategic planning; a desire to be all things to all people ("mission drift") or a failure to adapt to community needs quickly (Ebarb 2019). Here, I make my own addition to the list: a failure to embrace technology or use it effectively, something I call tech proficiency failure.

Arthur had, in fact, asked an important question: *How big is too big?* I spent the rest of the evening mulling the question while sipping my bourbon. When I delivered my usual report to the board the following month, I was able to say with amusement:

> Arthur asked an interesting question last month. He asked, "How big is too big?" I want to thank him—and each of you—for challenging me to think about that. Here's my answer, and I think Arthur's point was that we can't properly serve our mission when we focus exclusively on size.…

How Big Is Too Big?

Four Secrets for Assessing Nonprofit Size

1. **QUALITY.** Quality comes first. Performance excellence and excellent service delivery can never take a back seat to ambitions of growth and expansion.
2. **TALENT.** To the extent that growth offers opportunity for team actualization, mission expansion, and greater excellence; and, to the extent that growth offers team members professional opportunity to

fulfill personal life goals and ambitions for advancement even while supporting the agency's mission and constituency with talent and creativity—then bigger can indeed be better.

3. **RESOURCES.** To the extent that growth allows a nonprofit to acquire the critical resources—funding, technology, facilities, investment—necessary to achieve, maintain, and advance its mission with excellence ... bigger can be better.

4. **CONTEXT.** When we ask, "How big is too big?" we really are asking: "Is bigger better?" For a nonprofit, success is measured via service excellence, mission scope and scale, and outcomes in a given community. For a nonprofit, merger matters only inasmuch as it can be leveraged for large-scale social change and improved community outcomes. Therefore, the critical measure of success for a nonprofit is not size but quality and excellence.

"The answer to Arthur's question, then, is, 'No. Bigger isn't better. *Better is better!*'" I looked directly at Arthur. He was beaming like a proud uncle. An excited murmur rose around the boardroom table. Folks were smiling and nodding. "Bigger isn't better," people were nodding with enthusiasm. "*Better is better!*"

"The challenge," I continued, "is how do we achieve excellence and stay excellent? If growth allows us to attain and maintain excellence while increasing our mission's scope and scale, then growth is not only good, it's the embodiment of what our founding families have charged us to do. For any other reason or purpose, bigger is *not* better. Bigger cannot be better because only *better is better*."

The best thing about excellence is that people *want* to be excellent. **Excellence serves the nonprofit mission, and it serves the aspirations of team members who want to do well by doing good.** Best of all, it serves the people and the communities that the nonprofit was established to support. When teams perform well and missions grow, communities thrive. Where communities thrive, individuals can flourish.

When people with IDD first began succeeding at The Arc's microbusinesses, learning valuable job skills and making friends, a transformation occurred. Folks we thought were barely verbal started talking—a lot! *Possibilities became fulfilled.* People began dressing with greater care and paying more attention to their grooming. This was not just true of the people we served. "I used to get up in the morning and wear any old thing," one longtime employee told me after a Day of Caring, a day when local businesses and the United Way of Southeastern Connecticut brought new furnishings and a fresh coat of paint to our headquarters. "But now, when I walk into this beautiful lobby, I feel I need to look my best, to be my best professional self."

The Arc ECT's embrace of excellence and its possibilities improved the agency's collective self-esteem and lowered the hurdle that a poverty of expectation had placed in our way. Before the mergers and strategic planning and transformational exercises, a lack of resources had led to a certain dinginess and sense of depletion agencywide. The low bar for housekeeping spilled over into our service delivery.

Well-trained teams delivering excellent services take pride in their professionalism and derive a healthy sense of professionalism from that process. Team members talk to one another, and it is common for direct support professionals and leaders at our agency, folks who've worked at other agencies in the past, to say thank you to The Arc ECT: Thank you for the opportunity; thank you for the respectful environment; thank you for the safe conditions and the technology and the supportive training and leadership. People who have worked elsewhere understand things are different at The Arc ECT, where we walk with the people we serve and the people who serve them In Partnership for Full Equality.

My office is next to one of the larger training rooms at the agency, which allows me to interact with new team members and say hello. Every now and then, as I make my way down the hall, I will hear a leader from one or another of our departments beginning his or her introduction even while closing the training room door. It always makes me smile when I hear these words: "We do things differently here."

At The Arc, we do things with excellence, with virtue. We do things as a team. This is what *In Partnership for Full Equality* really is all about.

Despite the thrill mergers can present, saying no to a merger at times might well be the wiser path to excellence. Following the successful completion of The Arc Quinebaug–New London County merger—and all the positive momentum and press that entailed—The Arc ECT was approached (and continues to be) by other agencies representing themselves as like-minded and likewise seeking partnerships of the sort they'd read about in the newspapers.

At such times, the first step is a highly preliminary one. Nondisclosure agreements (NDAs) are signed ensuring that confidential data and intellectual property shared cross-agency will remain private for all concerned. Next, the conversations begin.

How might you know that a merger isn't a good idea? For merger to succeed, excellence (or the potential for it) must be a demonstrated, shared value.

And so it happened that Laura Shaw*, our own board president, and I walked into a meeting with a local agency that had approached The Arc ECT to discuss potential partnership. There, at the end of a long mahogany table, sat the executive director of Agency Artful* along with the agency's new board president, Mabel Watkins* … the latter absolutely glowering.

We had not met Mabel before; indeed, she had just been installed as Agency Artful's new president. (The prior board president had made the initial contact with us.) I asked if their team had any questions, and Mabel said, "Well, you're the only guys we're interested in talking to!" Noting we found that to be good news, I said: "Potentially, I think we both could enjoy highly positive results via partnership." Mabel cut me off. She continued to scowl, informing us that she had done "many, many, many" mergers in her day as a for-profit textile industry executive*.

Hearing that, I apologized obsequiously, saying: "Clearly you have superior knowledge!" The irony was lost on Mabel, who continued to elucidate on her vast merger experience. When she finished, I nodded and pointed out the advantages of technology and shared talent that partnership frequently brings, but Mabel waved her hand, her brow fixed. "I know how it works," she said. "You save money by laying everybody off! I have done this many, many, times!"

Laura, The Arc's board president, leaned forward. "But we've never laid anyone off in a merger," she said.

"Mergers are a great source of talent," I said. "Besides, there's a direct support professional shortage out there. Lay people off, and you'll never see them again!"

But Mabel's train of thought had barreled off to the next station in her mind. She was growing ever more agitated. I tried to reassure her.

"We have saved big money post-merger not by laying people off but by investing merger savings into technology." Mabel waved her arm, "We're not interested in that!"

"Are you interested in any kind of partnership?" I asked. Mabel jumped in her seat. "Yes!" she thundered. I asked if Agency Artful had an interest in microbusiness development, and again Mabel waved her hand dismissively saying: "We aren't interested in that."

So, I asked Mabel what, if anything, she wanted to discuss. Was there something else Agency Artful wanted to accomplish today? Still glowering, Mabel said she couldn't think of anything.

We stood, and I handed Mabel the requisite pack of Classic Crunch Chocolate Chip cookies. She smiled for the first time and said she'd been looking forward to getting a pack as she'd heard they were delicious. Then, with her executive director in tow, Mabel bustled out of the room and headed down the stairs and out the door.

Laura looked at me, and I at her. We laughed. "I guess she's going to teach me how to do a merger!" Laura smiled.

"It appears she intends to teach me too!" I said.

Agency Artful's executive invited me to coffee a few weeks later. Over warm drinks, the executive expressed deep concerns about the funding landscape. The Arc ECT was not too troubled by it, given the success of our Voter Guide and our cash position vis-à-vis our most recent merger. I said as much and added that I believed we'd managed to defy industrywide instability with mergers, which had brought welcome resources and stability. I noted that larger agencies had clout that smaller ones did not these days, and we felt fortunate to qualify as being among the former now.

The executive looked as though he had something else to say. I waited. "Ignore Mabel," he said, "she's just … Mabel…."

But we at The Arc ECT knew that if Mabel was determined to flex the muscle of the smaller organization in ways that jeopardized the core values of The Arc ECT, then we were not going to be able to ensure excellence for anybody—not for the people we serve, for their families, nor for the members of either team. As a courtesy, we met one more time, again at Artful's request. During this meeting, per prior agreement, each team laid out some of the important systems we'd built and discussed how we had done it and to what advantage; we asked operational questions of one another.

The Arc ECT team was curious. Mergers set the stage for new ways of thinking, bringing new ideas forward and new opportunities for streamlining and embracing and enhancing organizational structure. Not every organization can wrap its arms around progress, however. The other team did offer a small complement of quality services, and we admired that and enjoyed hearing the details of those operations. But when The Arc's team laid out its own systems, it was as if an absent Mabel had channeled herself back into the room.

These were systems Artful had indicated in the first phone call, one they had initiated, that they needed and felt would benefit them in a partnership or possible merger. Now, we were told, "We don't need that," or, "we already do that!" Perhaps Agency Artful had built a whole new infrastructure in the last 60 days, but that was unlikely.

"How do you manage to keep your Special Services department profitable?" asked one of Artful's young executives. "We use technology," I told him.

"We don't need that," he replied.

Agency Artful's team also seemed oblivious to the value of leading with a gift. Indeed, despite the NDA, in the ensuing months, some ideas we had shared in our meetings were put forward in community discussions as Agency Artful's ideas. Since we weren't interested in providing a brain trust sans reciprocation, we simply stopped pursuing a partnership.

When does a nonprofit say no to partnerships and/or merger? Here is The Arc ECT's checklist.

When Is Bigger Better? A Guide …

1. **MISSION REINFORCEMENT.** Will this alliance reinforce the mission of your organization? Will it strengthen your organization's core values? Will it allow for mission growth and improved quality? Will it lead to excellence and better services for the greater community (*i.e., Is it better for the people you serve and for your team*)?

2. **OVERREACH.** Is the other organization offering a chance to expand services? Are the services an appropriate extension of your current

platform or an expansion that will overtax the surviving entity? Is the other organization stable economically and reputation-wise or will it bring liability to one or both organizations' missions? Does the other agency bring to the table values and resources that will afford both groups long-term, lasting strategic advantages? What are they? If the other organization (or your own) possesses areas of instability—will the surviving entity have the resources to turn things around?

3. **CULTURE.** Does the culture of the presenting nonprofit offer opportunities to reinforce the positive aspects and aspirations of your own? Does the organization possess good ethics? Is the organization open to excellence as a value? Is there potential for facilitating both teams toward a shared Vocabulary for Change? For problem solving? For creating greater quality and excellence? Will a partnership enhance your reputation or give you an opportunity to rejuvenate lackluster services? If not, excellence requires that you pass.

The Arc ECT is in the empowerment business. Aligning ourselves with an agency that embraces a business model with an incurious mindset isn't something our board, our constituents, or our team want or need. Excellence requires a disciplined embrace of virtue and shared values.

Incompatible culture is widely regarded as the No. 1 reason that mergers fail. One party's inability to add value to the deal, paying too much, or moving forward when one or both parties are undercapitalized are some others. I have seen mergers fail for all these reasons. Even when culture is not a sticking point, The Arc ECT has balked in cases where we would have acquired large properties requiring deep resources for maintenance and upkeep.

Indeed, Southwest Airlines received a nod earlier in this book for its impressive stock gains since inception, but an additional caution around mergers/acquisitions surfaced following the carrier's holiday meltdown at 2022's year end. Some employees and analysts blamed the airline's troubles, in part, on growth (via merger/acquisition) and a failure to sustain that growth with tech investment.

"It is the complete failure of Southwest Airlines executive leadership," complained the president of the flight attendants' union, Lyn Montgomery. "It is their decision to continue to expand and grow without the technology needed to handle it (Sider 2022). Southwest acquired Trans Star (formerly Muse Air) in 1985; Morris Air in 1993; and Air Tran Airways in September 2010. Given that the company continues to rank first in customer satisfaction in the J.D. Power North American Airline Satisfaction Study among economy airlines (Sider 2022), it's unlikely Southwest's mergers/acquisitions will cause it to fail. The carrier's experience—contrasted with its successes—serves as a cautionary tale, nonetheless: Transformation, with or without mergers, must be ongoing for every organization.

Maintaining excellence requires a principled, constant focus on investing in people, services, technology, and outcomes. It requires doing so even while emphasizing strategic planning, goal setting, goal attainment—and, yes, profit. For a nonprofit, however, profit is a different kind of success marker than it might be for a Fortune 500 corporation or other business. Profit, for a nonprofit, is a measurement of mission strength and fulfillment, outcomes, fiscal resilience, and excellence. It's important that nonprofit teams experience a multifaceted exposure to excellence. Nonprofit teams need to inherently understand that bigger isn't better—better is better.

Surveys tell us that profit and money are not the primary motivators of any workforce. *Entrepreneur* magazine points out that opportunity, vision, creative potential, and the employer's genuine interest in employee well-being, cross-sector, are the primary drivers of workforce retention and performance (Basgall 2015).

Given a choice, most employees choose fulfillment and excellence over cash. One caution here is that, *especially for nonprofits*, fair pay and arbitrary layoffs do matter—particularly when funders begin to take a hard-working, well-trained workforce for granted as Connecticut once did. For a leader, be it nonprofit or for-profit, to stand in solidarity with the team she leads on matters of wages and other important issues is reflective of the kind of leadership this book espouses.

To achieve and maintain excellence, it is necessary to inspire your team emotionally and motivationally; the best leaders actively use the resources at their disposal to encourage and enable people to reach ever higher levels of performance and professional satisfaction. **The best leaders look for ways to say yes.**

When the COVID-19 pandemic struck, The Arc ECT's frontline leaders provided their teams with daily, positive messaging, along with incentives ranging from special dinners and gift cards to hazard pay based on risk, from amounts of 7 to 100 percent per hour (double-time). We certainly were not the only nonprofit doing this.

Other responses that team members told us they appreciated included CEO memos of support weekly and informational podcasts. Along with real information about COVID-spread statistics and tips for practicing safe behaviors, the memos and podcasts we produced contained information from webinars with the CDC and other credible scientists. Board members sent e-mails of support to the team. Central to every message was a collective goal: Let's keep the people we serve safe; let's keep the people who serve them safe (our workforce); let's keep our own families—yours and mine—healthy. We made a commitment to truth. And, as we know, truth builds trust.

Throughout the pandemic, individual team members at all levels of the organization were urged to put the personal health and safety of themselves and their families first, and to check in with leadership and let us know how they were doing. The heartfelt messages I received from our team helped my own family and myself keep our spirits higher during some very grim times.

Our direct support professionals and mid-level leaders thanked us, their leadership team, for the investments we made in protective equipment and hazard pay. As America became a nation awash in the divisive messaging of a politicized pandemic, The Arc ECT's podcast audiences swelled. Eastern Connecticut itself had come to see The Arc ECT as a trusted, reliable source of empowering information.

Excellence as virtue, like truth, nurtures trust. And excellence, by virtue, is inclusive. Exclusion is, if nothing else, a vacuum of limited perspective.

As this book nears completion, The Arc ECT is partnering with several leading regional nonprofits, the Southeastern Connecticut Council of Governments, the Community Foundation of Eastern Connecticut, The Chamber of Commerce of Eastern Connecticut, United Way of Southeastern Connecticut, the NAACP, major regional employers and industries, educational institutions, service clubs such as Rotary International and local municipalities, to create a nonprofit brain trust in Eastern Connecticut.

Just as President Franklin Roosevelt assembled America's best and brightest during World War II, Eastern Connecticut has embarked on a collaboration to create a mentoring partnership to guide the region's most talented residents toward nonprofit board service. A curriculum, youth outreach, trainings, and more are being assembled to the benefit of our region's nonprofits. At the heart of the effort lies the goal of expanding board representation. Excellent boards are inclusive boards, reflective of their greater communities. When excellence in leadership prevails, excellent results follow.

Excellent leaders attract and retain diverse and excellent talent at every organizational level. Excellent leaders listen to the voices who bring their talents to bear in support of the organization's mission. Indeed, these are the voices that will ultimately safeguard the very mission and reputation of the organization.

Even when a team is excellent, when it thinks it is doing everything right, even when a team theoretically *is* doing everything right, a smart and excellent team is trained to understand that the unexpected does occur. However diligent you and your team might be, unanticipated crises will occasionally arise. At such times, you cannot afford to function in the vacuum of limited perspective.

Unforeseen events, and missteps too, while potentially embarrassing, offer your organization an opportunity to listen better and then to demonstrate responsibility, accountability, and integrity (virtue!). Consider that some folks might have seen an international pandemic approaching, but most of us did not. Under ordinary circumstances, people—even well-trained, well-intended professionals—do fail to anticipate the unknowable. The more diverse your team, the better prepared you will be to anticipate, learn, adapt, and respond.

What do you do if the unexpected happens and a public spotlight of scrutiny falls upon your organization? Be it an international or national crisis or the most basic failing of human nature on a local scale—an ability to face the unexpected with a well-crafted plan rooted in excellent habits is key. Here is The Arc ECT's blueprint for demonstrating excellence in crisis management.

Successful Crisis Management as Plan A

1. **TAKE RESPONSIBILITY.** Briefly and without making excuses or verbally rambling around, acknowledge the problem.
2. **DEMONSTRATE ACCOUNTABILITY.** Indicate that you and your organization are taking full responsibility to address the challenges posed by the situation at hand.
3. **TAKE CORRECTIVE ACTION.** Broadly and cleanly, outline your plan to remedy the situation.
4. **LOOP BACK TO REPORT PROGRESS.** Report back at promised intervals on the progress of your corrective response, and report on the positive results thus far. It's OK to briefly note a few challenges faced along the way and how these were overcome as well.

Here again, truth builds trust. Accountability is the foundation upon which nonprofits build a reputation for excellence, merit a community's good will, and better serve their public. Accountability is not just an external exercise. A driving force behind The Arc ECT's 2020–2023 Strategic Plan was, in fact, accountability and empowerment on the part of the agency's leaders toward the people we serve and to our team. Wise nonprofit boards hold themselves and their nonprofit leaders accountable.

After the New London/Quinebaug merger, in the middle of the pandemic, a Gallup-licensed workforce consultant administered an employee satisfaction survey agencywide. In doing so, leadership demonstrated its own accountability to the team in accordance with the strategic plan. The C-Suite volunteered to undergo 360 executive assessments in which team members who report to us provided feedback on our leadership performance. In the Gallup survey, The Arc ECT's team gave its leadership a 4.5 out of 5 score for keeping the team safe during the pandemic and for creating a positive environment postmerger. This vote of confidence came just one year after the merger.

Growing your brand and awareness of it along with high expectations for your organization's accountability and trustworthiness need not be an expensive endeavor. It need only be a planful, deliberate effort informed by the *11 Secrets of Nonprofit Excellence*. Among those secrets is having a strategic plan for your agency's long-term excellence. The same plan will provide excellent direction, too, for confronting the unexpected quickly and on the fly if necessary. Excellence requires a commitment to establishing a safe space to create and to listening to diverse voices. Only with perspective can an organization deliver excellence consistently and virtuously. After all, bigger is not better—better is better.

Excellent nonprofits are all about giving back and paying it forward. Excellent nonprofits lead with graciousness. Besides offering community partners packages of chocolate chip cookies, The Arc ECT leads with a gift in other ways, too.

For more than a decade now, we have printed simple note cards with our logo and an inside message that reads: "*Congratulations on your milestone. The Arc Eastern Connecticut celebrates accomplishment in our community.*" The cost of this gesture is less than $1. Over the years, some of the most wonderful letters of thanks we have received have been in response to our congratulation notes. Messages from community leaders who have received our cards include police officers, other nonprofit leaders, local human rights icons, private businesspeople, politicians, social workers, and even city planners. So many of them (too many!) have said: "*No one ever thanked me for my service before.*"

True excellence marries your mission benevolently with community need. The purpose of those cards, initially, was to educate people about The Arc, to remind the community at large that *every person, including each person with IDD, brings a gift of ability to the community.*

We never dreamed a simple card would end up being so much more than a simple educational tool. Over time, the cards have become vehicles of inspiration encouraging Eastern Connecticut's leaders themselves to persevere along their own journeys of excellence. Serendipitously rather than strategically, the cards have opened many doors for the agency and the people we serve.

Excellence is self-fulfilling. Nonprofit excellence fuels community excellence. Excellent communities nurture better, more virtuous human beings. Virtuous human beings build and maintain excellent, inclusive social constructs. Such habits build a powerful, self-fulfilling momentum: inclusion plus transformation equals excellence. In Partnership for Full Equality indeed.

The Secrets of Chapter 11

- CULTURE IS A CRITICAL ASPECT OF SUCCESSFUL MERGERS. Only the type of growth that reinforces core values and leads to mission expansion with excellent results can serve a nonprofit. Will your mission be stronger? Will your values be bolstered? Will you attain the resources of excellence as well as further inclusion and equality for the people you serve? Will this, in turn, reinforce your organization's ability to grow excellently? Remember: Facilitated discussion (and listening!) are critical for reinforcing a positive team culture and a shared Vocabulary for Change and collaboration.

- MONEY IS JUST ONE FACTOR IN EMPLOYEE RETENTION. Vision, creative potential, the employer's genuine interest in team well-being, and professional development—these are the drivers of workforce retention. That said, nonprofit leaders cannot allow funders to take advantage of their teams' dedication and good intentions.

- CRISIS MANAGEMENT IS A CRITICAL EXERCISE IN EXCELLENCE. Take responsibility; demonstrate accountability; take corrective action; report back on progress. Ensure that your team is reflective of the community you serve and the people your mission embraces so your ability to listen and respond appropriately is credible and well-informed.

- GROWING YOUR BRAND AND EXCELLENCE NEED NOT BE AN EXPENSIVE ENDEAVOR. Lead with a gift, the simpler and more gracious the better.

- **IS BIGGER BETTER? No! Better is better!**

For Discussion

- ARE YOU SATISFIED WITH YOUR ORGANIZATIONAL CULTURE? What do you like about it? What needs to improve? In what ways is it inclusive? In what ways is it not? Make a list of three initiatives that will help move your team and your services closer to a measurable, excellent, more inclusive environment. **Are there community partners with whom you can work to strengthen both your missions and brands in complementary ways—both in the nonprofit and for-profit sectors? Make a list, pick up the phone, and set the meetings in motion.**

- HOW CAN YOU BEST RETAIN TALENT? List one thing you can do to connect your organizational mission to your team's professional aspirations. (Note: Asking your team how you can help them to do so is great place to start!) How will this exercise reinforce your mission and your agency's quest for inclusion, empowerment, and excellence?

- DO YOU HAVE A CRISIS MANAGEMENT PLAN? What is it? Remember a crisis from the past. Using the principles of crisis management as a measure of excellence, how would you respond today?

- LEAD WITH A GIFT REDUX. What are some simple, yet gracious actions that you and your team can take to build community goodwill? What will be your processes for rolling these out and ensuring they are ongoing and inclusive?

Bibliography

Administration for Community Living, U.D. 2001. *Sexual Abuse.* Disability Justice. https://disabilityjustice.org/sexual-abuse/#:~:text=Approximately%20 80%25%20of%20women%20and,assaulted%20more%20than%2010%20 times (accessed August 18, 2022).

Aristotle. 1941. R. McKeon, ed., *Nicomachean Ethics.* New York, NY: Random House.

Basgall, J. June 8, 2015. *Great Employees Don't Work for Just Pay. They Need Much More.* Entrepreneur. www.entrepreneur.com/article/246678 (accessed December 12, 2020).

Brooks, S.A. April 7, 2015. *Southeastern Connecticut Economy Gets Low Marks in National Report.* Fox 61. www.fox61.com/article/news/local/outreach/ awareness-months/southeastern-connecticut-economy-gets-low-marks-in-national-report/520-917332f7-ac22-4dd1-8d9b-4dba17b3d478 (accessed September 29, 2020).

Collins, J. 2005. *Good to Great and the Social Sectors* 15. Boulder, Colorado: Jim Collins.

Daily Mail. 2015. *Cookie Monsters!* DailyMail.com. www.dailymail.co.uk/femail/ article-3346769/Cookie-monsters-average-American-adult-eats-19-000-sweet-treats-lifetime-chocolate-chip-revealed-country-s-favorite-flavor.html (accessed September 19, 2020).

Department of Developmental Services. 2009. *Community Living Arrangement Licensing Report.* Hartford: State of Connecticut.

Desilver, D. August 29, 2019. *10 Facts About American Workers.* Pew Research Center. www.pewresearch.org/fact-tank/2019/08/29/facts-about-american-workers/#:~:text=More%20than%20157%20million%20Americans, assembly%20lines%20and%20checkout%20counters (accessed August 28, 2020).

Duffin, E. July 2, 2019. *Nonprofit Organizations in the U.S.—Statistics & Facts.* Statista. www.statista.com/topics/1390/nonprofit-organizations-in-the-us/ (accessed August 28, 2020).

Ebarb, T. 2019. *Nonprofits Fail—Here's Seven Reasons Why.* National Association of Nonprofit Organizations & Executives. NANOE. https://nanoe.org/ nonprofits-fail/ (accessed November 17, 2020).

Edmondson, A.C. 2012. *Teaming.* San Francisco, CA: John Wiley & Sons, Inc.

Encyclopedia Britannica. 2020. *Brain Trust.* www.britannica.com/topic/Brain-Trust.

Gallo, C. June 20, 2012. "Steve Jobs' Four Magic Words That Built Pixar." *Forbes*. www.forbes.com/sites/carminegallo/2012/06/20/steve-jobs-to-pixar-chief-just-make-it-great/#24b06980252e (accessed August 11, 2020).

Grant, R.M. 2016. *Contemporary Strategy Analysis*. Sussex, United Kingdom: Wiley.

Harvard University Business School. June 25, 2020. *Nonprofit Crisis Management Workshop*.

House Congressional Record. 1955. *101, Part 3*, p. 3451. Washington, DC.

Independent Sector. 2020. *The Charitable Sector*. Independent Sector. https://independentsector.org/about/the-charitable-sector/#:~:text=The%20nonprofit%20sector%20%E2%80%93%2010%20percent,2.7%20percent%20increase%20from%202015 (accessed August 28, 2020).

International City/County Management Association. 2005. *Effective Supervisory Practices*. Washington, DC: International City/County Management Association.

Jandernoa, B. 2010. *Leading for Profound Change and Innovation*. Reno Nevada.

Larson, E. September 21, 2017. "New Research: Diversity + Inclusion = Better Decision Making at Work." *Forbes*.

Leonard, H.B. 2018. "The Strategic Challenge." *Strategic Perspectives in Nonprofit Management*. Cambridge: Harvard University Business School.

London, M. January 21, 2016. "Geraldo: The Story 'Branded on My Soul' That Caused a Revolution." *Fox Nation*. Fox News Channel. www.foxnews.com/media/geraldo-willowbrook-branded-my-soul-fox-nation (accessed May 5, 2020).

Mary Raum, P. 2013. "Steve Jobs: From Lumbini to Kushinagar." *Academia*. www.academia.edu/6768379/CaseStudySteveJobs (accessed August 11, 2020).

McMillen, S.P. 2014. *The Economic, Fiscal and Social Impacts of Health & Human Services Public Charities in New London County, Connecticut*. United Way of Southeastern Connecticut, The Community Foundation of Eastern Connecticut and The Chamber of Commerce of Eastern Connecticut.

Merger Remarks. January 3, 2019. Danielson, Connecticut.

Messier v. Southbury Training Sch., No. 3:94-cv-01706 (VAB) (D. Conn. August 31, 2018). 2018.

National Coalition for the Homeless. 2009. *Employment and Homelessness*. Washington, D.C.: National Coalition for the Homeless. www.nationalhomeless.org/factsheets/employment.html (accessed October 20, 2020).

National Public Radio. March 7, 2008. *Remembering a New York Institution*. National Public Radio. www.npr.org/templates/story/story.php?storyId=87975196.

Nazar, J. October 8, 2013. "14 Famous Business Pivots." *Forbes*. www.forbes.com/sites/jesscollen/2020/06/30/bookingcom-is-a-trademarkdoes-this-matter-to-your-business/#482b0a4f331f (accessed July 14, 2020).

Perry, R. January 20, 2016. *When Do You Say No to a Donor?* Veritas Group. https://veritusgroup.com/when-do-you-say-no-to-a-donor/#:~:text=You%20 say%20no%20when%20a%20donor%20wants%20to,to%20further%20 the%20interest%20of%20a%20business%20partner (accessed September 2, 2020).

Peters, T.J. and R.H. Waterman, Jr. 2006. *In Search of Excellence.* New York, NY: Collins Business Essentials.

Phaneuf, K.M. August 6, 2018. "For Connecticut's Nonprofits, A Time of Reckoning." *The CT Mirror.* https://ctmirror.org/nonprofits/ (accessed October 3, 2020).

Phaneuf, K.M. July 17, 2019. *Wall Street Agency Warns CT's Battle With Pension Debt Is Far From Over.* CT Mirror. https://ctmirror.org/2019/07/17/wall-street-agency-warns-cts-battle-with-pension-debt-is-far-from-over/ (accessed September 28, 2020).

President's Committee for People with Intellectual Disabilities. 2017. *Report to the President 2017: America's Direct Support Workforce Crisis.* United States Department of Health and Human Services.

Rivera, G. January 5, 2016. *The Story That Revealed Willowbrook's Horrors.* (R.P. Roman, Interviewer). New York. www.pbs.org/video/metrofocus-story-revealed-willowbrooks-horrors/d.

Scharmer, C.O. 2018. *The Essentials of Theory U.* Oakland, CA: Berrett-Koehler Publishers, Inc.

Sharplin, A. September 3, 2020. *Strategic Planning Process.* EDUCBA. www .educba.com/strategic-planning-process/ (accessed 2020).

Shellenbarger, S. October 9, 2019. "The Best Bosses Are Humble Bosses." *The Wall Street Journal.*

Sider, A. December 28, 2022. "How Southwest Airlines Melted Down." *Wall Street Journal.*

Stauffer, K. 2014. *Nonprofit Organizations: How Big Is Too Big? A Discussion of Structure, Quality and Transformation.* Class Paper, Mystic.

Stauffer, K. July 14, 2020. "It's About Saving Lives." *The Bulletin.*

Stauffer, K. June 26, 2019. *From Courage to Cookies*, pp. 4–6. Norwich, Connecticut: Kathleen Stauffer.

Stauffer, K. n.d. *Muhammad Ali.* https://bykathleenstauffer.com/muhammed-ali/ (accessed June 29, 2020).

The Arc Eastern Connecticut. January 21, 2020. *Strategic Plan 2020-2013.* Norwich, Connecticut; Bruce Putterman, facilitator.

The Cravory. 2016. *Fun Facts About America's Favorite Cookie.* https://thecravory .com/blogs/the-cravory-the-ultimate-cookie-experience-1/123677505-fun-facts-about-americas-favorite-cookie (accessed September 19, 2020).

The Walt Disney Company. 2013. "The Disney Institute." *National Conference of Executives of The Arc.* Orlando.

The Walt Disney Company. n.d. https://thewaltdisneycompany.com/about/#:~:
text=The%20mission%20of%20The%20Walt,the%20world%27s%20
premier%20entertainment%20company (accessed June 24, 2020).

U.S. Census Bureau. 2020. *Population.* Washington, D.C.: U.S. Census Bureau.
www.google.com/publicdata/explore?ds=kf7tgg1uo9ude_&met_y=population
&idim=country:US&hl=en&dl=en (accessed August 28, 2020).

United States Department of Transportation. n.d. *The Emergency Shipbuilding
Program.* Maritime Administration. www.maritime.dot.gov/content/emergency-
shipbuilding-program (accessed 2020).

University of Minnesota. 2018. *How Many People in the United States Have IDD?*
(R.I. Project, Producer). RISP. https://publications.ici.umn.edu/risp/2018/
infographics/people-with-idd-in-the-united-states-and-the-proportion-who-
receive-services (accessed August 27, 2022).

University of Pennsylvania. n.d. "Tipping Point for Large-Scale Social Change."
ScienceDaily. doi:www.sciencedaily.com/releases/2018/06/180607141009
.htm.

Wehmeyer, M.L. 2013. *The Story of Intellectual Disability.* Baltimore, MD: Paul
Brookes Publishing Co.

Weissmann, J. April 28, 2014. *The Decline of Newspapers Hits a Stunning Milestone.*
https://slate.com/business/2014/04/decline-of-newspapers-hits-a-milestone-
print-revenue-is-lowest-since-1950.html (accessed August 29, 2020).

WVIT NBC Connecticut. March 20, 2020. *Governor Lamont Orders Non-
Essential Businesses Closed; Urges Residents to Stay Home.* Hartford-New
Haven, Connecticut. www.nbcconnecticut.com/news/coronavirus/gov-lamont-
to-provide-update-on-connecticut-coronavirus-cases/2242239/.

About the Author

Kathleen Stauffer is a strategic, results-driven professional with deep expertise in executive leadership and mergers/acquisitions. An expert on high-performance team building, organizational transformation and leveraging mergers for large-scale social change, she's enjoyed success as a CEO, president, division chief, and media group publisher. Under her leadership, The Arc Eastern Connecticut grew from a struggling $5 million nonprofit supporting people living with intellectual and developmental disabilities to an enterprising, $22+ million hybrid. Kathleen serves on national and regional boards and is a recognized leader, writer, and presenter.

Index

www.ingramcontent.com/pod-product-compliance
Lightning Source LLC
Chambersburg PA
CBHW061214220326
41599CB00025B/4636